"Finally—a user-friendly, step-by-step workbook on how to overcome panic disorder for teens and their families. The authors provide readers with everything they need to take control of their lives with this straightforward, comprehensive, and personal guide."

—**Bradley C. Riemann, PhD**, clinical director of CBT services at Rogers Memorial Hospital

"*The Panic Workbook for Teens* is an outstanding workbook that offers instant help and hope for teens suffering from panic attacks. Well written and chock-full of useful ideas and strategies, this book is a must-have for any teen seeking to conquer panic. Highly recommended!"

—**Kevin L. Gyoerkoe, PsyD**, director of The Anxiety and OCD Treatment Center in Charlotte, NC, and author of *10 Simple Solutions to Worry*

"This workbook is loaded with examples of how real-life teenagers have used and benefited from CBT-based treatment for panic disorder. Readers will benefit from the simple and easy-to-implement action steps outlined in this workbook. In addition, the mindfulness-based perspective highlighted in the text should assist readers in learning to live more fully in the moment, even if panic occasionally comes along for the ride."

—**Mark B. Powers, PhD**, licensed psychologist and research associate professor in the Anxiety and Health Behaviors Lab within the Institute for Mental Health Research

"What a great book for teens looking to overcome panic disorder! The authors have distilled the best of the cognitive behavioral approach to panic and condensed it into forty short recovery tools with brief instructions and exercises. These powerful, precise, and pragmatic steps will save you lots of research and searching. Get your folks a copy as well!"

—**David Carbonell, PhD**, author of *Panic Attacks Workbook* and the "coach" at anxietycoach.com, a popular self-help website

the panic workbook for teens

breaking the cycle
of fear, worry &
panic attacks

DEBRA KISSEN, PhD
BARI GOLDMAN COHEN, PhD
KATHI FINE ABITBOL, PhD

Instant Help Books
An Imprint of New Harbinger Publications, Inc.

Publisher's Note

This publication is designed to provide accurate and authoritative information in regard to the subject matter covered. It is sold with the understanding that the publisher is not engaged in rendering psychological, financial, legal, or other professional services. If expert assistance or counseling is needed, the services of a competent professional should be sought.

Distributed in Canada by Raincoast Books

Copyright © 2015 by Debra Kissen, Bari Goldman Cohen, and Kathi Fine Abitbol
Instant Help Books
An Imprint of New Harbinger Publications, Inc.
5674 Shattuck Avenue
Oakland, CA 94609
www.newharbinger.com

Cover design by Amy Shoup
Acquired by Tesilya Hanauer
Edited by Gretel Hakanson

Library of Congress Cataloging-in-Publication Data on file

Printed in the United States of America

17   16   15

10   9   8   7   6   5   4   3   2   1   First printing

To all of our fabulous clients, you inspire us with your strength and honesty. We are honored to serve as your guides past anxiety.

—Debra Kissen, PhD;
Bari Goldman Cohen, PhD;
& Kathi Fine Abitbol, PhD

Contents

Acknowledgments

To Morton Kissen, my father, friend, and colleague.

To Marsha Kissen, you are forever with me.

To Jordyn, Jakob, and Morgan, you fill my life with delight.

To Jonathan, you have taught me the meaning of family, and for that I will be forever grateful.

To Bug Jen, you have done more than anyone to help me walk through and eventually past my anxiety. You taught me that even in the most brutal moments of life, you can still find tenderness and joy if you are open to them.

Nathalie, my soul sister, thank you for always understanding me, even when I don't understand myself.

Judy, you inspire me with your clarity of thought. I am so lucky to have you in my life.

With eternal love,
Debra

To my parents, Henry and Marilyn Goldman, for your unconditional love and support.

To my husband Matt, for your ever-present patience, love, and level head.

To my kids, Madden and Hadley, for your spunk and wit. Thank you for bringing such joy into my life.

To my brother, David Goldman, for your guidance and intellect.

With all my love,
Bari

To my incredible parents, Shari and Mark Fine, and Evelyne Abitbol, for your endless encouragement, faith in my abilities, and love.

To my husband, Jeremy Abitbol, you always keep me laughing and have won my heart for eternity.

To my siblings, Jeff, Karen, Kevin, and Kristin Fine, Adam and Lisa Brody, and Jonathan and Stephanie Abitbol, you are terrific role models and always cheer me on.

To my nephews and niece, Josh, Zach, Andrew, Justin, and Brendan Fine, and Stephanie, Dylan, and Ryan Brody, you are all very talented and make me so proud.

To my friends GG Collins, Ashley Freeland, Lauren Huffman, Kat Makielski, Paula Sklar, Lauren Stone, and Tamra Wallerstein, for all of your support and our momentous adventures together.

All my love,
Kathi

Introduction

When I was nineteen years old, I began to experience strange, terrifying sensations that appeared to show up out of the blue. I tried to ignore them, but they only got worse. I tried to fight them, but they only grew. I did not want anyone to know how scared I was for fear that I would appear weak, or worse, "crazy."

At that time, I was able to "white knuckle" my way past panic disorder and push myself forward despite the discomfort. I only wish someone had informed me that I was suffering from panic disorder and that this was, in fact, one of the most treatable mental health conditions. One painful side effect of my undetected panic disorder was that I came to believe there was something wrong with me. It seemed to me that in some core way I was broken or lacking, and that was why I was experiencing such disturbing sensations.

If only I could time travel back to 1996. I would educate my young self on the physiology of panic disorder and explain to her in simple terms why she was experiencing those disturbing sensations. I would assure her that she is whole and of sound mind and, in fact, is brave and powerful. I would let her know that she has so much to look forward to, such as meeting her wonderful husband, raising three delightful (and often exhausting) children, and a flourishing career as a clinical psychologist. Unfortunately, it took me almost ten years to accidentally stumble upon the most empirically supported treatment for panic disorder, cognitive behavioral therapy (CBT).

My colleagues—Dr. Bari Goldman Cohen and Dr. Kathi Fine Abitbol—and I wrote this workbook with the goal of introducing CBT for panic disorder in order to expedite your journey to finding the most effective treatment for panic disorder. We are honored to be your guides through and soon past panic disorder.

Warmest regards,

Dr. Debra Kissen

panic 101

As you kick off this journey past panic, it is important to first figure out if you are actually having panic attacks, if you have panic disorder, and whether or not it makes sense to seek out professional help in addition to using this book. This activity will help you answer all these questions. ·

for you to know

A panic attack is a period of intense fear that occurs suddenly and seemingly out of the blue. During a panic attack, you may experience any combination of the following feelings:

- A feeling of immediate danger or doom

- An intense need to escape

- Heart palpitations

- Sweating

- Trembling

- Shortness of breath or a smothering feeling

- A feeling of choking

- Chest pain or discomfort

- Nausea or abdominal discomfort

- Dizziness or light-headedness

- A sense of things around you being unreal

- Feeling unreal

- A fear of losing control or "going crazy"

- Fear of dying

- Tingling sensations

- Chills or heat flashes

for you to do

First, let's determine whether or not you have ever had a panic attack.

Have you ever had an abrupt onset of intense fear?

Yes   No

If yes, what symptoms have you experienced?

A feeling of imminent danger or doom

An intense need to escape

Heart palpitations

Sweating

Trembling

Shortness of breath or a smothering feeling

A feeling of choking

Chest pain or discomfort

Nausea or abdominal discomfort

Dizziness or light-headedness

A sense of things around you being unreal

Feeling unreal

A fear of losing control or "going crazy"

A fear of dying

Tingling sensations

Chills or heat flashes

Did you circle at least four of the above?

Yes   No

If no, you may not have experienced a full-blown panic attack, but that does not mean panic is not showing up in some form and that you won't benefit from the activities in this book.

If yes, do the panic attacks ever occur without any external cues that one is about to happen? For example, is it seemingly out of the blue with no rational explanation attached?

Yes   No

If yes, you likely have experienced at least one unexpected panic attack. If no, you likely have experienced expected panic attacks.

Next, let's determine whether or not you meet the criteria for panic disorder. The main symptom of panic disorder is extreme fear of experiencing future panic as well as avoidance of life activities that might bring on more panic. In other words, panic disorder entails panicking about panic or feeling anxious about the sensations of anxiety.

Do you experience persistent and typically unanticipated panic attacks?

Yes   No

If yes, do you have a continual fear of future attacks, or do you avoid participating in any important life tasks to limit panic symptoms?

Yes   No

If yes, has the fear or changes in behavior occurred for at least one month?

Yes   No

If you answered yes to these three questions, you likely have panic disorder.

Summary Assessment

For the following questions, give an answer from 0 through 10 (0 being not at all, 10 being extreme):

In the past week, how uncomfortable did panic sensations make you? _____

How much distress do you feel about having panic symptoms? _____

How much do you avoid activities and other aspects of life to avoid panic? _____

How would you rate your overall life satisfaction? _____

more to do

Your safety is always the top priority. To determine whether you should seek professional help in addition to self-help, please answer yes or no to the following questions.

Have you checked in with a physician to rule out medical causes for your symptoms?

Yes   No

If you have not reported your symptoms to a physician, we recommend you discuss what you are experiencing with a physician before proceeding with this workbook. It is always good to get clearance from a doctor before proceeding with a self-help initiative.

Do you feel that your symptoms cause medium to high levels of discomfort? (Is at least one area of your life—social, school, work, and so forth—currently at a medium difficulty level?)

Yes   No

Do you have a desire to engage in self-harm behaviors such as cutting?

Yes   No

Do you have consistent suicidal thoughts?

Yes   No

Are you using drugs or alcohol to cope with negative emotions?

Yes   No

Do you have moderate to frequent feelings of hopelessness?

Yes   No

If you answered yes to any of the questions above, it is recommended that you seek professional help. You may find professional help by asking for a referral from a friend, family member, or doctor, or through a trusted organization such as the Anxiety Depression Association of America (http://www.adaa.org).

Regardless of your responses to these questions, your anxiety made you uncomfortable enough to pick up this workbook. Even if you do not meet the criteria for panic disorder, you need not feel burdened by your panic and anxiety. Everyone deserves to be in control of his or her anxiety. Props to you for taking this first step forward, past your panic!

2 reading about panic makes me panic

If reading about panic makes you feel panicky, you are not alone. It is super common for those struggling with anxiety to avoid getting help because they are too afraid to admit they are struggling. By reading about anxiety and panic, you are actually taking the first step in moving beyond it, by facing what you fear head on.

for you to know

This workbook will discuss different exposure-based exercises you can engage in to reduce the role of panic in your life. You are in fact engaging in your very first exposure, at this very moment. By reading about PANIC PANIC PANIC PANIC PANIC, you are training your brain to chill out and not get so freaked about PANIC PANIC PANIC PANIC PANIC. It is just a five-letter word. It can't hurt you. You are safe and sound, even if you are sitting here reading and thinking about PANIC PANIC PANIC PANIC PANIC.

for you to do

Get out your timer. For the next two minutes, you are allowed to think about anything you want except for a pink elephant. However, if your mind happens to offer up anything having to do with a pink elephant, make a tally mark on the page. Keep track of the number of intrusions that occur over the two-minute period.

How did you do? Could you avoid thinking about pink elephants for two minutes? Most likely not. This is because the more you tell yourself not to think of something, the more it will come to mind. Therefore, the more you tell yourself that it is possible to avoid anything and everything associated with panic or anxiety, the more you will think about panic and anxiety. Even if you are successful for a little while, the thoughts will always come back and will be stronger with each avoidance effort.

more to do

Every day, expose yourself to a few words associated with anxiety. Instead of avoiding, keep looking at the words and track your anxiety level. See how long it takes to decrease by half. Start with writing a few words that make you anxious and look at them continuously. Notice if your anxiety level decreases over time. After reading the words successfully, try saying words associated with anxiety and panic symptoms out loud.

3   the body on panic

It is time to take the mystery out of a panic attack. Without understanding your body "on panic," all you know is that your body and mind feel completely out of whack and something feels terribly wrong. One of the most liberating steps in moving past panic is to put your scientist cap on and learn about the physiology of panic.

for you to know

All the uncomfortable sensations of panic actually have a vital purpose in protecting you from an immediate threat.

Panic Sensation	Why is my body feeling this way?
Feeling dizzy and disconnected from reality	These sensations are due to overbreathing. When faced with an imagined threat, the body takes in excess oxygen to power up muscles to flee from danger.
Tingly, cold hands or feet	Your hands and feet may feel tingly and cold due to blood flow being redirected from your hands and feet to muscles more critical to survival, like those in your arms and legs.
Blurred or altered vision	Your pupils may dilate in order to better perceive danger. This can make your vision extra sensitive to stimuli in your visual field.
Foggy head or difficulty concentrating	This is due to decreased blood flow to the head and increased blood flow to muscles required for survival such as your arms and legs.

Increased sweating	Sweating cools your body off so you don't overheat. An additional benefit of sweating is it makes you slippery and therefore difficult for an angry predator to grasp.
Upset stomach	You may be feeling nauseated or experiencing other symptoms of an upset stomach due to blood flow being redirected from your digestive system to other parts of your body. After all, it's no time to digest a big meal when you are about to be someone else's meal.
Difficulty breathing	To fuel up for battle, your body takes in extra oxygen (hyperventilating). Taking in so much oxygen and breathing out so much carbon dioxide can create a smothering feeling.
Heart racing	In the face of danger, your heart beats faster to supply more oxygenated blood to your vital organs to fuel you up for battle
Feeling shaky	To assist you in escaping from danger, your body releases the hormone epinephrine (also known as adrenaline). Adrenaline directs blood to your muscles to power you up for the fight of your life. The increased blood flow to your muscles may leave you feeling shaky.

for you to do

Draw your own body on panic. Where do you feel your panic? Color the areas of your body where panic sensations most often show up.

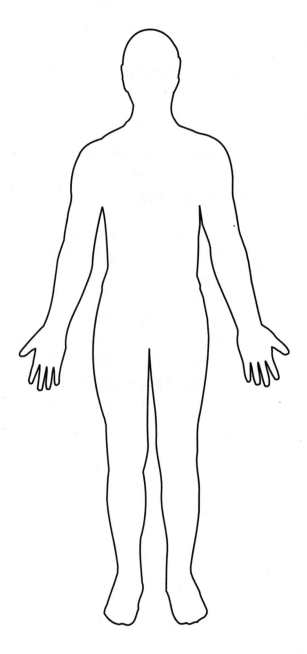

Have you ever experienced the following sensations when having a panic attack?

Sensations of Panic	Yes or No
Feeling dizzy and disconnected from reality	
Tingly, cold hands or feet	
Blurred or altered vision	
Foggy head or difficulty concentrating	
Increased sweating	
Upset stomach	
Difficulty breathing	
Heart racing	
Feeling shaky	
Feeling hot or increased sweating	

Next, for all sensations you have experienced, note the level of discomfort or fear you experienced when feeling the identified sensation. Also note your initial interpretation of the sensation (for example, when feeling a tightness in your chest, perhaps you had the thought "What if I am having a heart attack?").

Sensations of Panic	Yes or No	Strength of Anxiety Associated with Sensation (on a scale of 0–10)	Interpretation of These Feelings (for example, "I am having a heart attack" or "I am going crazy")
Feeling dizzy and disconnected from reality			
Tingly, cold hands or feet			
Blurred or altered vision			
Foggy head or difficulty concentrating			
Increased sweating			
Upset stomach			
Difficulty breathing			
Heart racing			
Feeling shaky			
Feeling hot or increased sweating			

more to do

On an index card, jot down all panic sensations you answered yes to above. For each physical sensation of panic, write down why your body feels this way, or the physiological explanation for this feeling. Use your own words to explain what is causing the panic sensation. How is this sensation part of a complex system, in place to protect you from immediate danger? The next time you are experiencing panic, review this index card and remind yourself why you are feeling what you are feeling. You may be thinking, "Okay. I get it. There's no reason to write it out when I already understand it." What you understand when you are sitting here calmly reading this workbook is very different from what you understand and believe to be true when you are having a panic attack. Trust us; this information will be much less accessible when in the midst of panic.

4 body awareness

Individuals struggling with panic disorder have a tendency to notice their body only when it is operating in full-blown panic mode. Learning how to observe and attend to your body before the onset of a panic attack is the key to preventing a panic attack from brewing.

ashley's story

Ashley was so consumed with panic that she rarely noticed much else going on in her body. One day, Ashley was sitting in history class when she began to feel strange sensations. Her head felt tight and tingly as though a band were wrapped around it. She was immediately seized by terror. She thought to herself, "Is this what it feels like to have a stroke?" She excused herself from class and went to the bathroom. She decided that if she was having a stroke, she would rather not have one in front of her classmates. While in the bathroom, she looked in the mirror to assess for signs of some awful neurological disease. All she saw looking back at her was her own face with a super tight headband on, which she forgot she had put on this morning.

for you to do

It is time to get to know your body when it is *not* on panic. Your body is not simply a storage unit for panicky feelings. There is a lot more going on than just panic sensations.

Take a moment to scan your body for all attention-grabbing sensations. Start with the top of your head. Notice any tension or tingling or heaviness. Next, move down to your face, your mouth, your nose, your forehead, and your ears. Next, notice your shoulders. Are they raised and tight, are they loose, or are they somewhere in between? Next, notice your chest and any heaviness or tightness that may be present. Continue moving down to your stomach, your arms, your hands, the feeling of your legs making contact with the seat or floor, and, finally, your feet. Now, notice any urges that may be showing up to change or rid yourself of the sensations you are having. You may be experiencing the desire to feel more relaxed or less tense. You don't need to change anything. Your only job right now is to make room for whatever it is that you are currently feeling.

Your homework for the next week is to do a body scan, as described above, twice a day, at a set time (perhaps once in the morning and once before bed). Your goal is to do this body scan based on the time you assigned to yourself, not based on the feelings of panic demanding to be attended to. Track your daily body scan practice with the log provided in this chapter.

Day and Time of Body Scan	Sensations Observed

more to do

Just because certain parts of your body are not filled with panic and screaming at you, demanding to be attended to, does not mean they are not worthy of a little TLC. Your homework this week is to pay attention to one non-panic-related body part a day for one minute. Follow the schedule below to reacquaint yourself with the body parts that aren't in the panic zone.

Monday: For one minute, focus your attention on a finger. When your mind wanders (which it will), gently guide your attention back to your finger.

Tuesday: For one minute, focus your attention on your ears. When your mind wanders (which it will), gently guide your attention back to your ears.

Wednesday: For one minute, focus your attention on your chin. When your mind wanders (which it will), gently guide your attention back to your chin.

Thursday: For one minute, focus your attention on your knee. When your mind wanders (which it will), gently guide your attention back to your knee.

Friday: For one minute, focus your attention on your elbow. When your mind wanders (which it will), gently guide your attention back to your elbow.

Saturday: For one minute, focus your attention on your nose. When your mind wanders (which it will), gently guide your attention back to your nose.

Sunday: For one minute, focus your attention on your lips. When your mind wanders (which it will), gently guide your attention back to your lips.

5 life through panic-colored glasses

At this very moment, you may be seeing the world through "panic-colored glasses." When wearing panic-colored glasses, everything appears dangerous and threatening.

evan's story

Evan was on winter break from college. He was having a fantastic freshman year. He was managing his academic workload with minimal stress. He felt on top of the world. And then one day, everything shifted. Evan was at lunch with some friends when out of nowhere, he began to feel a deep sense of dread. The walls of the restaurant felt like they were caving in on him. The lights appeared too bright, and he felt disconnected from his environment. He felt like he could not take a deep breath, and he was having pains in his chest. He felt a sensation of impending doom, as though the end were somehow near.

Evan told his parents about the awful feelings he was having, and they quickly got him an appointment with a psychologist. In the first session, the psychologist explained that Evan was having a panic attack. The psychologist asked Evan to draw a picture of what he felt like when he was having a panic attack.

After that, Evan's psychologist asked him to draw a picture of what he sees and how the world looks when wearing panic-colored glasses.

for you to do

In the space below, draw a picture of yourself seeing the world through panic-colored glasses. What do you look like? Where do you hold the tension in your body? How is your posture? Are you standing tall or crouched over? Are your shoulders up to your ears or down?

Next, draw a picture of what you see when wearing panic-colored glasses. How does the external world look? What colors come to mind? How do other people appear?

more to do

The next time you are having a panic attack, try to muster the energy to go to a computer and pull up any news website. Write down the first three headlines that grab your attention when you're wearing panic-colored glasses:

1. _____

2. _____

3. _____

Next, find a time when you are feeling relaxed and comfortable. Try the same exercise as described above. Go to a computer and pull up any news website. Write down the first three headlines that grab your attention when you're *not* wearing panic-colored glasses:

1. _____

2. _____

3. _____

Compare and contrast the headlines that grabbed your attention when you were wearing panic-colored glasses, versus what grabbed your attention when feeling relaxed and comfortable. Do you notice any patterns?

6 the flip side of panic is excitement

> The same body sensations are felt in times of panic and moments of excitement. Body sensations are not "good" or "bad." It is how we think about these sensations that causes us to label them as "good" or "bad."

shari's story

Shari's freshman year in high school was filled with firsts. Two of these new experiences included falling in love and having her first panic attack. Falling in love came first. Shari met Mark in her history class. She noticed that whenever she was around Mark, her heart would pound and she felt a bit nauseated. On her first date with Mark, Shari noticed her palms sweating, difficulty catching her breath, and a hint of light-headedness. But Shari could not have been any happier. She wrote off those sensations as just excitement about such an important evening.

A month into Shari's romance with Mark, he broke up with her. Shari had a difficult time concentrating at school, and her grades began to slip. One Tuesday morning, out of nowhere, Shari had her first panic attack. She remembers first noticing that her palms and face were sweating, and her heart was pounding. She told herself, "This is so gross and weird. I hope no one sees me like this." When Shari next felt her heart pounding, she thought, "I am having a heart attack! This is awful. I can't handle feeling like this."

for you to do

List the sensations Shari felt during the following situations:

A. falling in love with Mark

_____

B. having her first panic attack

_____

What were Shari's interpretations of why she was having these sensations in situation A and in situation B?

A. falling in love with Mark

_____

_____

B. having her first panic attack

_____

_____

more to do

Guess whether the following quotes describe what it feels like to fall in love or what it feels like to have a panic attack.

1. "A wave of emotion moved through me so aggressively and intensely that I felt like I could not catch my breath."

2. "I wanted to run and hide. I felt like I could not handle how out of control I felt."

3. "I felt confused and disoriented. The wave of emotion that rolled over me felt raw and dangerous."

Answer key: 1. Love 2. Love 3. Love

For each example below, take a guess as to what the person is doing and what the person is feeling:

Example: Andrew's heart was pounding out of his chest, and he could barely catch his breath.

Andrew is taking a <u>test</u>, and he is feeling <u>terrified</u>.

Josh felt his cheeks flush, and he experienced churning in his stomach.

Josh is _____, and he is feeling _____.

Dylan's stomach was in his mouth, and his head spun.

Dylan is _____, and he is feeling _____.

Did you associate these situations with fear or positive emotions? What you did here may reflect your automatic response to interpreting attention-grabbing bodily sensations.

Next, try to consider possible neutral or positive explanations for these sensations and write these down as well.

Example: Andrew's heart was pounding out of his chest, and he could barely catch his breath.

Andrew is _dancing to his favorite song_, and he is _feeling elated_.

Josh felt his cheeks flush, and he experienced churning in his stomach.

Josh is _____, and he is feeling _____.

Dylan's stomach was in his mouth, and his head spun.

Dylan is _____, and he is feeling _____.

How do you feel after considering positive explanations?

Next, circle all of the panic-related body sensations that you have felt recently in the left column below. Include any additional sensations. Then to the right, write a neutral or positive situation when you or someone else may have had that same sensation.

Panic-Attack Sensation	Neutral or Positive Situation When Same Sensations Could Be Experienced
Heart palpitations	
Sweating	
Trembling	
Shortness of breath or a smothering feeling	
A feeling of choking	
Tightness in chest	
Nausea or abdominal discomfort	
Dizziness or light-headedness	

A sense of things around you being unreal	
Feeling unreal	
Feeling out of control	
Tingling sensations	
Chills or heat flashes	
Other (write in your own):	

Notice how the same sensations can be interpreted as scary or normal and even good. Next time you are having panic, remind yourself, "I *can* handle these feelings, and in a different situation, I wouldn't even mind (and may even like) them!"

7 it's only a false alarm

The brain is always scanning for danger. Sometimes it misfires and determines one is in danger when one is actually safe and sound. A panic attack is simply a false alarm going off in your brain.

for you to know

Have you ever accidentally set off the smoke detector? Perhaps you were making yourself a meal or attempting to surprise your parents with a birthday breakfast. You were innocently placing French toast on the grill when all of a sudden a ton of smoke arose from the frying pan, setting off the smoke alarm. And thank goodness for that smoke alarm because if there had been a real fire, you could have quickly left the premises and gotten yourself to safety. But when trying to make yourself an after-school snack and your relaxing moment is interrupted by the obnoxious sound of a smoke alarm, the smoke detector is more annoying than helpful. Similarly, a panic attack is a false alarm going off in your brain.

for you to do

Let's play a game of Danger Versus False Alarm. For the situations listed below, specify whether they represent an appropriate time to experience the panic response or a false alarm.

- You are taking an important exam and begin to feel hot and flushed.

- You are driving on the highway and notice your heart rate accelerating.

- A fire breaks out in your home.

- A lion lunges for your face.

- You are at a party with friends and begin to feel weird and out of it.

- You are about to step on a rattlesnake.

- You are walking up a flight of stairs and have a difficult time taking a deep breath.

Think of three times in your life when the panic response was of assistance to you and protected you from danger. Now think of three times when the panic response was a false alarm and was more annoying and uncomfortable than it was helpful.

more to do

The next time you notice panic surfacing, play a game of Where Is the Danger? Do a quick *true* danger assessment:

1. Are there any angry bears approaching?

2. Am I standing in the midst of a fire?

3. Do I see any armed gunmen?

4. Is there a volcano erupting before my eyes?

5. Is the ground shaking due to an earthquake?

6. Is hail coming down from the sky (or locusts or angry wasps or other dangerous flying objects)?

Add your own *true* danger assessment question.

7. _____

If the answer to any of these questions is yes, immediately put down this workbook and attend to the emergency at hand. If the answer to these questions is no, then remind yourself that panic is a false alarm going off in your brain.

Next, respectfully inform your brain that until you observe any of the previously listed dangers, you are going to stay put and teach it that it is (and you are) actually safe.

For the next week, for all panicky moments, jot down your initial anxiety level. Then, play a quick game of Where Is the Danger? and look around the room for any imminent threats. Finally, jot down your anxiety level after playing Where Is the Danger? (If you need more room, you can download additional copies of this chart at http://www.newharbinger.com/32219. See the very back of this book for instructions.)

Day and Time	Initial Anxiety Level (0–10)	Where Is the Danger? Questions Posed	After Where Is the Danger? Anxiety Level (0–10)

Create a coping card to remind yourself that a panic attack is simply a false alarm going off in your brain. Be as creative as possible. Try drawing a picture that represents this concept. Where can you keep this coping card so that this concept is handy and accessible when you need it most?

8 from panic to panic disorder

The main differences between people who have an occasional panic attack and those who meet criteria for panic disorder are how much they fear the experience of panic and how much they alter their life to avoid experiencing panic.

jillian and samantha

Jillian and Samantha sat next to each other in freshman English. One day tornado sirens sounded, and the students were instructed to crouch down and cover their heads with their hands. The power in the building flickered on and off, and strong winds could be heard outside. Jillian started feeling her heart race and began to sweat. She felt dizzy and experienced stomach pains. Her thoughts were racing. All she could think about was when this storm would be over. Samantha was equally terrified. She was feeling shaky and having difficulty breathing. Her heart was pounding, and she had constant chills.

Soon the sun reappeared, class resumed, and life returned to normal. Samantha focused on her schoolwork and her friends and rarely thought about how scared she had felt during the tornado warning. In contrast, Jillian continued to feel afraid. While she knew that her initial feelings of panic were caused by the tornado warning, what she did not know was when or if she would ever feel that awful again. She found herself constantly scanning her body to assess if she was having a hard time breathing or if her heart rate was increasing. She was constantly thinking of ways to avoid feeling panicky. Jillian began feeling hopeless. The harder she tried to not feel panic again, the more she panicked.

for you to do

On average, this week, how many hours a day did you think about panic? _____

Put a check mark next to the thoughts and behaviors below that you experienced when thinking about panic.

☐ Thoughts related to how much you hate panic

☐ Thoughts related to how much you dread feeling panic

☐ Thoughts related to how bad it will be if you start to feel panic

☐ Scanning your body to determine if you are starting to feel panic

☐ Thoughts related to how nice life was before you had panic

☐ Trying to figure out what is wrong with you

☐ Contemplating if you will ever get better and stop feeling so awful

☐ Other: _____

Over the past week, what activities did you avoid in order to prevent experiencing panic?

_____

_____

Based on your own experience, does thinking about how much you hate panic and avoiding certain activities assist you in getting rid of panic?

more to do

For the next week, any time your mind decides to think about how much it hates panic, grab your brain's remote control and change the channel. You can change it from PANIC NEWS to any other channel. Think about sports, think about friends, or look out the window and observe the marvels of nature. It does not matter what channel you put on, as long as you redirect from PANIC NEWS to any one of the millions of potential channel offerings available in your mind. Does panic really deserve any more of your attention? Hasn't it wasted enough of your time already?

mindfully attending to panic thoughts

There is a middle ground, somewhere between running from panic thoughts and clinging to them, which entails mindfully attending to them. Mindfully attending to thoughts means observing all thoughts, whether we consider them good or bad, with an open, accepting attitude.

for you to know

Now it is time to discuss a tricky nuance. In activity 2, we told you that the more you try not to think about panic, the more you will end up thinking about panic. In activity 8, we told you to grab your brain's remote control and change your mind's channel from PANIC NEWS to any other station. What gives?

We don't want you to have to run from panic thoughts, but we also don't want you locked into panic thinking. Peace is found somewhere between these two extremes. Freedom from panic thoughts can be obtained by learning to mindfully attend to those thoughts and then to redirect your attention back to the present moment or to whatever *you* choose to focus on (versus what panic wants you to focus on).

for you to do

Zoe was sitting in class, listening to her teacher review the material that would be on the final. She began to feel a weird tingly feeling in her hands; thinking about a recent news story on warning signs of an impending stroke, she tried to remember whether tingly hands was one of the signs. The more she tried to assess whether she was having a stroke, the worse she felt. She spent the remainder of class in "panic land" and only heard bits and pieces of the information her teacher was saying.

Mary was sitting in class, listening to her teacher review the material that would be on the final. She began to feel a weird tingly feeling in her hands; thinking about a recent news story on warning signs of an impending stroke, she tried to remember whether tingly hands was one of the signs. She soon caught herself getting stuck in panic thoughts. She gently reminded herself, "I am having the *thought* that I am having a stroke. This does not mean I am actually having a stroke." She then used all of her strength to redirect her attention back to what her teacher was saying. A few minutes later, stroke and panic thoughts resurfaced, and she once again practiced noticing the thoughts and labeling the thoughts. She then redirected her attention back to what the teacher was saying. By the end of class, she had practiced gently redirecting her attention more times than she cared to count, but the good news was that she spent only a few minutes in total engaging with panic thoughts. For the majority of class, she was listening to her teacher and obtaining the information she needed for her final.

Compare how Zoe related to her panic thoughts to how Mary related to her panic thoughts.

Who spent more time following panic's lead, Zoe or Mary?

Who was able to get more out of her class period?

If you could offer advice to Zoe to help her attend less to panic and more to her teacher what would you tell her?

more to do

For the next week, set a five-minute time period to practice mindfully attending to *all* thoughts. For the practice period, your job is to focus your attention on your breath and think "in" on the in breath and "out" on the out breath. Every time your attention wanders off, notice the thought that grabbed your mind's attention, describe the thought ("I just had the thought that this is stupid" or "I just had the thought that I am thirsty"), and then return your attention back to your breath. The goal of this exercise is not to relax you but rather to strengthen your mind's ability to redirect attention back to the current moment.

For the following week, practice mindfully attending to all panic thoughts. Whenever you notice that a panic thought has surfaced, your job is to follow the four steps to mindfully attending to panic thoughts below.

1. Notice when a panic thought surfaces. Try to observe panic thoughts with an accepting, curious attitude.

2. Label the panic thought. Instead of telling yourself, "I am losing my mind," tell yourself, "I am having the panic thought that I am losing my mind."

3. Redirect your attention back to the present moment or whatever it is you choose to attend to.

4. Repeat as needed, every time a panic thought shows up.

Fill out the chart below every time you practice mindfully attending to a panic thought. Additional copies of the chart, if you need them, are available at http://www.newharbinger.com/32219.

Date and Time	Panic Thought	Was I able to label panic thought? (Y/N)	Was I able to redirect my attention back to current moment? (Y/N)

A panic attack is not a "thing," but instead it is a dynamic process made up of inter-connected thoughts, feelings, and behaviors.

for you to know

The three components of a panic attack are body sensations, thoughts, and behaviors. Body sensations include feelings such as heartbeat, sweating, shaking, shortness of breath, nausea, dizziness, and feelings of suffocation. Thoughts include anything that we think or tell ourselves. Behaviors are the actions we do. (But note that not doing something and remaining still is also a behavior.)

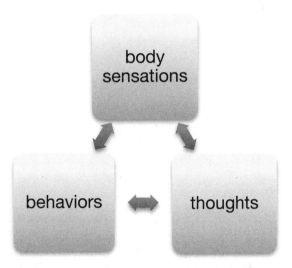

Each of these three parts can affect the others. Your body sensations can affect what your thoughts are, and your thoughts can bring on or affect your body sensations. Your thoughts can affect your behaviors, and your behaviors can affect your thoughts. Your behaviors can affect your body sensations, and your body sensations can affect your behaviors.

for you to do

Imagine you are at a frozen yogurt place. Instead of creating the perfect frozen yogurt, though, we would like you to create the "perfect panic attack." Take your time reading the lists of "ingredients," and notice how each of them could potentially contribute to a panic attack. Please circle the top two ingredients in each category that you believe would be the best at creating the biggest and worst panic attack for you. Just like with choosing frozen yogurt toppings, there is no right or wrong answer. The ingredients for creating your perfect panic attack are different from what it would take for Joe Schmoe to experience a panic attack that would rock his world.

Body-sensation ingredient choices:

Fast heart rate or pounding heart

Sweating or chills

Shaking

Shortness of breath

Feeling of choking

Nausea or butterflies in stomach

Dizziness or light-headedness

Feeling out of control or feelings of unreality or being detached from yourself

Numbness or tingling sensations

Add your own:_____

Thought ingredient choices:

I am not okay.

I absolutely can't do this.

It is not okay to have panic in front of others.

It is not okay if people judge me.

I need to be as perfect as I can.

I can't handle it if people are mad at me.

I am not capable of handling this.

I will never get better.

No one understands.

I am losing control.

People can tell that I am not okay.

Add your own: _____

Behavior ingredient choices:

Avoiding things that are difficult

Avoiding things that are scary

Avoiding places that may increase your panic

Procrastinating on doing necessary tasks

Staying in bed

Avoiding people

Leaving places early when you feel uncomfortable

Asking other people to do things for you

Asking others if you are okay

Making decisions based on your panic

Drinking alcohol or self-medicating in some other way

Add your own: _____

more to do

Think of your most recent panic experience. List as many of your own body sensations, thoughts, and behaviors as you can remember having:

Body sensations:

_____

_____

_____

_____

Thoughts:

_____

_____

_____

_____

Behaviors:

_____

_____

_____

_____

Next, draw your responses using the panic-cycle model below, showing how each sensation, thought, and behavior may possibly affect and be affected by the others. Feel free to draw as many arrows as you like in as many directions as you want.

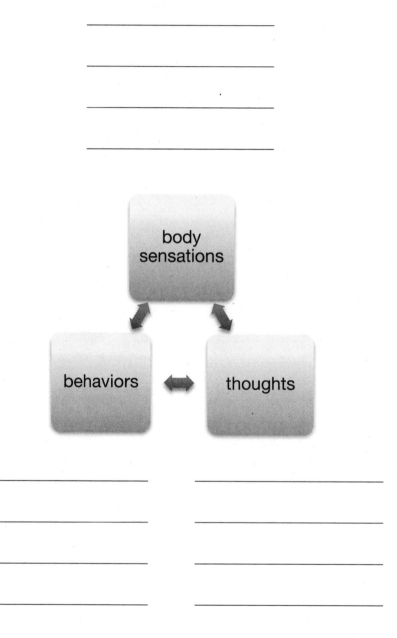

tracking panic

Paying attention to, or "tracking," panic helps you stop feeling like a prisoner to your panic. Instead, you'll feel like a detective trying to solve a case.

jeremy's story

Jeremy's therapist assigned homework to Jeremy that asked him to track his panic symptoms. Although at first collecting the data made Jeremy feel even more anxious, in time tracking his panic attacks became a helpful habit. By writing down the different elements of his panic attacks, Jeremy was able to view more objectively what was happening to him and felt more distance from his scary thoughts and feelings. In addition, he was better able to think through what he could do to move through the uncomfortable, panicky moment.

for you to do

Think about the last time you experienced a panic attack or a period of heightened anxiety. Use that last memory to write down, or track, the following information. It is okay if you do not remember all of the details; just write down the basic facts that you recall. It is okay to feel anxious thinking about and writing down these answers.

1. What was the day of the week? _____

2. What was the time of day? _____

3. What you were doing when the panic started? What were you doing during the panic episode?

   _____

   _____

4. What thoughts were going through your head when the panic started? And what thoughts did you have during the panic episode?

   _____

   _____

5. What physical sensations was your body feeling? Which of these did you not like?

   _____

   _____

6. What was the intensity of the panic on a scale of 0 to 10 (10 being the worst panic you've ever had)? _____

7. How long did the panic last? _____

more to do

Analyze the data.

1. Is there something about this day that usually brings on your panic?

   _____

2. Is there something about this time that usually brings on your panic?

   _____

3. How was your overall stress that day?

   _____

4. Can you think of any additional components to the panic, such as a poor night's sleep, an increase in caffeine intake, relationship challenges, hormonal shifts, and so on?

   _____

5. Did anything you do, in reaction to the panic, assist in decreasing the intensity and duration of the panic attack?

   _____

   _____

6. Did anything you do, in reaction to the panic, lead to an increase in the intensity and duration of the panic attack?

   _____

   _____

7. As you conduct this post-panic-attack analysis, can you think of anything you
    could have done differently to decrease the discomfort and distress associated
    with this panic attack?

    _____

    _____

    _____

    _____

reward yourself 12

Fighting panic is difficult and exhausting. Obviously the ultimate reward is to feel better. However, it is also helpful to earn short-term rewards to keep you incentivized as you move toward your long-term goal of freedom from panic.

jennifer's story

Jennifer was really motivated to fight her panic. She was sick of feeling fearful and allowing panic to run her life. Her ultimate goal was to reduce her panic to a bare minimum and to return to her "pre-panic" lifestyle. Jennifer considered herself to be really hardworking and persistent. She figured that if she just pushed herself each day, then she would be feeling back to normal in no time. However, after a few weeks of hard work, she started to feel tired. While she could acknowledge that some things were better, there was still a lot panic showing up in her life. She wanted to give up. Instead, she decided to break her ultimate goals into smaller, more tangible targets. Each time she met one of her smaller goals, she allowed herself to download a new song from iTunes. Just knowing that she would have a new song to listen to at the end of each week kept her going even when she felt run down. Each time she listened to the new songs, she remembered that she was making progress and that it wouldn't be long until she beat panic.

for you to do

Think about the recent jobs that you have done (babysitting, chores, and so on). What motivated you to do these jobs? If you knew that you were going to get paid something (even a small amount) versus nothing, how likely would you be to show up? Most teenagers and adults need some compensation to be motivated. In order to do difficult tasks, rewards are important, if not necessary.

Now make a list of possible rewards. You can keep a running list on Pinterest of things that you like, make an Amazon wish list or an Excel spreadsheet, or just write it all down on your hand. It doesn't matter how; just make a list. It shouldn't be hard to come up with things that would be meaningful to you!

Once you have determined your first reward, set a short-term goal that you need to meet in order to earn it.

more to do

Periodically revisit your list. Are the items you picked motivating enough? Have you been earning them? If not, then brainstorm other ideas for rewards. Keep setting small, short-term goals that are attainable.

healthy competition 13

You have to listen to your parents, and you have to listen to your teachers, but you don't have to listen to your panic. In fact, challenging your panic is the key to moving past it.

joe's story

Joe loved basketball. On the court he was aggressive and always went after the ball. However, when it came to panic, he did whatever it asked. After weeks of feeling beaten down by panic, he decided to treat it as an opposing basketball team. Joe realized that he would never just hand the ball over to an opponent and duck so that the other team had a clear shot of the basket. He knew that he would continuously lose the game if he did that. Recently, he had been just giving his panic the ball and giving it free rein of the court.

This all changed when he set up a healthy competition between panic and himself. Instead of handing over the ball, he fought. He did the opposite of what the panic told him to do despite feeling afraid. Each time that he challenged panic, he gave himself one point (two points if it was really hard). Whenever he gave in to panic, he awarded it points as well. At the end of each week, he tallied up the points and always aimed to come out on top. This really helped him gain perspective over the fact that the panic was separate from him and that while he couldn't control whether or not he felt it, he had a choice of how he handled it. Most times he chose to fight back and not give in to panic's demands. However, Joe knows that even though he is a great basketball player, he can't block every shot or make every basket. He used this realistic attitude to give himself a break when he couldn't push back against panic 100 percent of the time.

for you to do

Come up with a name for your opposing team (panic). On a piece of paper or a whiteboard (or on your computer) set up two sides by drawing a line down the middle. One side is for you, and one side is for your panic. Make sure that you use something meaningful to you and pick a situation where winning is important. Each time you fight or give in, make sure to award the proper team points. At the end of each week, tally up the points and see who won. If you came out on top, give yourself one of the rewards you came up with earlier in the book. You can create slogans, team names, and team colors. The more you get into the competition, the more likely you will continue to fight.

more to do

Keep a weekly "me versus panic" log to track what you were able to fight and when you had a harder time. Set the situations that were harder as goals for the following week and award yourself an extra point when you push back against panic in these more challenging scenarios.

the dreaded party guest 14

While living a panic-free life is ideal, there are going to be moments when panic rears its annoying head. When panic does show up, it is important to continue to participate in the activities most important to you, even if that means panic comes along for the ride.

for you to know

Imagine you are throwing a party and you found out that your best friend invited another friend that you don't really like. You have three choices: you can tell your friend to disinvite this guest, you can cancel your party to avoid seeing this person, or you can nod and say hi when the person arrives and then focus on the people that you do want to see at the party. When you walk by this unwanted guest, you can give a quick smile of acknowledgment, but you don't have to stop and chat. You don't have to be rude or ignore him or her, but you don't have to give him or her too much attention either. This is how you need to treat your panic. While it is not wanted, you can't push it away. Instead you can allow it to come along for the ride. But panic only gets shotgun. No need to hand it the keys and let it drive you away from everything important to you.

for you to do

Imagine that you are at a concert with your favorite band and the people next to you are being really obnoxious. Are you going to start a fight and try to make them change their behavior? Are you going to leave the concert to avoid having to listen to the annoying people? Or are you going to try to focus on the music and enjoy it? While you can't control the disruption, you can control how much you allow it to interfere with your enjoyment.

Now, notice a sound in the room that you didn't notice two minutes ago; how loud does it sound now? How loud was it before you actively paid attention to it? Notice how the noise was there the whole time, but since your attention was on something else, you didn't really notice. Now that you noticed it and are focusing on it, does it seem louder or quieter?

Finally, focus for one minute on something annoying around you (such as a sound or a smell). Then spend five minutes redirecting your attention away from the annoyance. Play a game on your phone, read a book, or do jumping jacks. After completing the distraction task, how annoying does the sound or smell seem now?

more to do

Next time you have a panic attack, set a timer and spend two minutes thinking about how bad you are feeling and how desperately you wish you were feeling differently. For the following two minutes, redirect your attention to anything else. Compare the discomfort you felt when you fully focused on how horrible it felt to have a panic attack with the discomfort you experienced when you actively attempted to redirect your attention to an external source.

no pain, no gain 15

There is nothing more effective at taking the wind out of the sails of panic than your ability to tolerate the sensations of anxiety. The more short-term discomfort you let yourself experience, the more long-term peace you will obtain.

for you to know

There are many examples of times in life where benefits are gained after enduring some amount of challenge or pain. One example is working out. Although there are ways we can have fun with exercise, there still is usually a challenge to our muscles. However, physical fitness tends to make us feel great and is usually thought to be worth the pain. The work you will continue to engage in throughout this book will lead to benefits beyond just fighting panic. The benefits will ripple to many important aspects of your life as you strengthen your ability to manage distress and ride out discomfort.

for you to do

Which of these discomforts are you willing to experience in order to no longer be held hostage by panic?

- Feeling the physical sensations of anxiety—such as a pounding heart, dizziness, nausea, and sweating—and allowing yourself to tolerate these sensations, in order to teach your brain that panic is uncomfortable but not dangerous:

  Yes   No

- Spending time in feared situations such as crowded places, social situations, and public speaking:

  Yes   No

- Feeling panic sensations and continuing to engage in daily activities:

  Yes   No

- Risk looking weird:

  Yes   No

- Tolerate feeling out of control:

  Yes   No

If you answered no to any of the questions, that is okay for now. Along your journey, if you are able to push yourself in any of the ways you didn't think possible, feel free to switch your answer at that time and consider it an even bigger accomplishment.

more to do

It is helpful to recognize and remember other successes you have had. These successes can be anything such as school accomplishments, work accomplishments, and personal goals.

List three things you have accomplished that you are proud of. No accomplishment is too small. Then, answer yes or no to the questions for each accomplishment.

1. Accomplishment: _____

    a. What effort, work, or pain was put in to succeed?

    _____

    b. Was the effort, work, or pain worth the emotional and tangible reward of success?

    _____

2. Accomplishment: _____

    a. What effort, work, or pain was put in to succeed?

    _____

    b. Was the effort, work, or pain worth the emotional and tangible reward of success?

    _____

3. Accomplishment: _____

    a. What effort, work, or pain was put in to succeed?

    _____

    b. Was the effort, work, or pain worth the emotional and tangible reward of success?

    _____

16 the cost of untreated panic

It is common for people struggling with panic to avoid important aspects of life in order to hide from panic. The challenge with this strategy is that panic is better at hide-and-seek than you are.

kyle's story

Kyle was at a movie premiere with some friends. About halfway through the movie, Kyle noticed that it was getting difficult to breathe. He tried to focus on the movie, but he was scared that he would stop breathing and kept thinking about his breath. He felt dizzy and out of it. His palms started sweating, and he felt as though he was losing control. Kyle felt that he could no longer stay in the theater. He ran out and called his mom to pick him up. While he was still upset and feeling sick, he also noticed the relief that he felt once he had left the environment where the symptoms started. Kyle wondered if he was getting sick and went to sleep. The next day his friends called him to hang out. His first instinct was to say yes, but then he remembered how he felt the night before. Kyle felt fine in the comfort of his own home and feared what would happen if he left. He declined the invitation and chose to stay home, where at least he felt safe. Over the next few weeks, Kyle avoided more and more situations that used to bring him joy.

for you to do

Put a check mark next to any situations you have avoided or would avoid in order to prevent experiencing anxiety sensations.

☐ Going to a party

☐ Going to the library

☐ Going on a date

☐ Sleeping over at a friend's house

☐ Attending a school function

☐ Attending a sporting event

☐ Going to work

☐ Going out to eat with friends

☐ Exercising

☐ Going to a movie

☐ Traveling via bus or train

☐ Driving a car

☐ Drinking coffee

☐ Riding an elevator

☐ Entering a crowded room

☐ Talking to new people

☐ Speaking in front of a large group

☐ Going somewhere a far distance from home

☐ Speaking on the phone

☐ Other: _____

_____

_____

more to do

Write down what activities you avoided in the last week in order not to experience panic.

_____

_____

Give a numerical rating of 0 to 10 to how much avoidance you engaged in during the last week (0 being none at all, 10 being the most extreme). _____

On average, how much anxiety did you experience this past week?

_____

Think back to a time before you experienced any panic. How many activities were you avoiding in order to not experience anxiety?

_____

How much anxiety were you experiencing at that time?

_____

How well is avoidance assisting you in not experiencing anxiety or panic?

_____

How distressed are you about missing out on events that you used to enjoy?

_____

For one situation you recently avoided, write a paragraph outlining what you fear would have happened if you had participated despite feeling panic.

_____

_____

_____

_____

_____

_____

17 don't go at it alone

There is nothing you need to hide about struggling with panic. Anxiety grows under the darkness of shame, and melts away when confronted with openness and acceptance.

stephanie's story

Stephanie remembers the exact moment when she mustered up the courage to tell others about her panic. Prior to that moment, she had tried for five months to deal with her panic symptoms on her own. She had always been taught that she needed to be self-sufficient. So even though Stephanie noticed weird anxiety symptoms ruining so much of her life, she held on tightly to the belief that she could make things better on her own. Late one Friday evening, however, this belief began to change. Her crush Zach asked her to prom. It was everything Stephanie had wanted, yet the word "no" came out of her mouth. Stephanie was very scared that if she went to prom, she would have a panic attack. The risk of feeling embarrassed in front of Zach and the other kids at school at a social event as big as prom was just too much to handle. Zach seemed surprised by the rejection but said, "no problem." Stephanie knew living like this was not okay. On Monday during second-period science class, she found out that Zach had asked Evelyne to prom on Sunday evening, and Evelyne had said yes. Stephanie's heart shattered. She finally accepted that trying to handle her anxiety on her own was not working. After science class was over, she texted her father to tell him she needed help. As Stephanie began treatment for panic disorder, she ended up also enlisting the help of her friends Justin and Ryan. With the support of her dad, Justin, and Ryan, Stephanie is now confident that when the next school dance comes around, she will be able to say yes.

for you to do

Identify all the people in your life who can be a source of support for you, for panic help or otherwise. We will narrow down your choice for panic support to one to three people in a bit, but first take a moment to think broadly about all the support people you have in your life. List as many people who might be there for you as you can think of. Your list can include friends, family, a therapist, and anyone else you feel close to. Your goal is to make the list as long as possible and to be reminded that you have a network of people who care about you.

_____

_____

_____

_____

_____

_____

Now, narrow your list to one to three people who can serve as supports for overcoming panic.

1. _____

2. _____

3. _____

more to do

Next, decide how you will let the people written above know about a) the difficulty you are experiencing, b) your goal to get past panic, and c) your desire to have them there for support if needed.

a. Circle any of the following phrases that you may use to explain the difficulty you are experiencing:

I have panic attacks.

I'm having symptoms such as _____.

I don't like these feelings, so I avoid certain situations.

These feelings are very difficult for me.

These symptoms make me feel _____.

I'm having a difficult time with my panic.

b. Circle any of the following phrases that you may use to explain your goal of getting past panic:

Panic disorder is treatable.

I have decided to address my symptoms.

To get over my panic symptoms, I am going to start addressing the problem.

I want to start treating my panic.

I am going to start confronting what makes me uncomfortable.

I am ready to move forward.

c. Circle any of the following phrases that you may use to explain your desire to have them there for support if needed:

I am hoping you can be there if I need your help.

Having someone there for support makes it more likely I will succeed.

Would you be okay with being a support for me?

I was wondering if you might be able to help me if I need it.

Treatment encourages me to have a support system, and I thought of you.

Is it okay if I ask you for help if I need support?

Now, using the examples that you circled above, attempt to write down a few sentences of what you would like to say to each of your specific support people. You are free to say anything you feel comfortable with, and you do not need to use any of the above examples unless they work for you.

1. _____

_____

2. _____

_____

3. _____

_____

18 create a panic-fighting mantra

In a calm, panic-free moment, it is easy to understand that a panic attack is simply a false alarm going off in your brain and you need not fear it. But in the midst of a panic attack, it is hard to think rationally. What you need in these high-panic moments is a simple anxiety-fighting mantra—a phrase you can repeat often that expresses your basic beliefs—to coach you through the discomfort.

steve's story

Steve began to see a therapist to help him move past panic. At the first session, the therapist explained that panic is like a greedy monster with an insatiable appetite. The greedy panic monster yells and screams, creating panic symptoms. The panic monster howls and harasses, until you give him a snack. The panic monster's favorite foods are avoidance and seeking out safety at all costs. When you give in to the panic monster and feed him a snack, he will quiet down for a short while. But he's really just digesting his snack and gaining more strength, so he can roar all the louder the next time he is hungry. The key to shrinking the panic monster down to a manageable size is to starve him of his favorite snacks—avoidance and safety-seeking behaviors.

After talking this concept through with his therapist, Steve came up with a panic fighting mantra: "Don't feed the panic monster." This mantra helped him ride out the short-term discomfort of a panic attack because it reminded him that by doing so he was actually starving the panic monster. He was then able to remind himself that it was actually a good thing to feel panicky sensations and do nothing to control them but instead to let them pass on their own. By staying put and attempting to engage in life as usual, he was making it more likely that he would experience less overall panic in the future. Steve held tightly to his panic-fighting mantra, and it got him through panic-filled moments that he never thought he would survive.

for you to do

Review the list of sample panic-fighting mantras. Put a check mark or an X next to each expression—a check mark if it's helpful, an X if it's not helpful.

☐ This too shall pass.

☐ What does not kill me, makes me stronger.

☐ I may not like this, but I can handle it.

☐ Bring it on.

☐ This is a false alarm going off in my brain.

☐ This is uncomfortable but not dangerous.

☐ I can ride this out.

☐ Just because I feel like I am going crazy, does not mean I am truly going crazy.

☐ I am okay; I just don't feel okay.

☐ Short-term pain, long-term gain.

Now, it is time for you to come up with your own panic-fighting mantra. What will speak to you is unique, based on your own biology and life experience. Your panic-fighting mantra may evolve and change over time. Just take a step back at this very moment and notice what your mind offers up. (Note that if you are in a negative mood and your mind is offering up mantras such as "Panic sucks, and I will never be free of it," you may want to take a break and come back to this exercise in a few hours.)

_____

_____

_____

more to do

Like any good tool, owning your panic mantra is only half the battle. You actually have to use it to benefit from its existence. The hardest part about using a panic-fighting mantra is that the times you need it the most are the moments when this material is the least accessible. Your brain will not offer up anything calming when in the midst of a panic attack. The only message your brain cares that you hear when knee-deep in panic is "A lion is about to eat your face. You better run for your life." Therefore, you need to rely on the assistance of your immediate environment to remind you of your panic-fighting mantra.

Think about the panic symptoms that you have experienced over the last few days. Where were you? What were you doing? For each of those panicky moments, think about how you could have best accessed your panic-fighting mantra.

Where was I when I experienced panic sensations?	What was I doing when I experienced panic sensations?	Where could I have accessed my panic-fighting mantra?

Check off three ways you will inject your panic-fighting mantra into your environment.

☐ Type and place my panic-fighting mantra somewhere readily available in my phone

☐ Place sticky notes in my home in the following spots: _____

_____

☐ Create a bracelet or some other form of jewelry that reminds me of my mantra

☐ Ask trusted friends and family to remind me of my mantra

☐ Record an audio or video message to myself, reminding me of my mantra and that I will survive whatever panic symptoms arise

☐ Send myself a text or e-mail, written at a calm moment, to be read in a panic-filled moment

☐ Draw a picture that symbolizes my mantra and carry this picture in my wallet, or take a picture of the image and keep it accessible in my phone

☐ Meet with a school counselor, let him or her know I experience occasional panic attacks, and if one happens at school, ask if he or she could remind me of my panic-fighting mantra

☐ Create a panic-fighting playlist to be accessible from my phone or computer

☐ Other: _____

Speaking of creating a panic-fighting playlist, music can do wonders in grounding you back in your body when you're feeling trapped in panicky thinking.

List your top three anxiety-fighting songs:

1. _____

2. _____

3. _____

How do these songs make you feel? If listening to your panic-fighting playlist makes you want to curl up in a ball and hide from the pain, reread this section and select a few different songs. If listening to your panic-fighting playlist elicits feelings of strength and hope, you are on the right track.

catastrophic thinking 19

We have certain thoughts that make us feel bad and are unhelpful to us. It is important to recognize when we have them and to understand why the thoughts are not entirely accurate.

for you to know

Our thoughts can play a large role in our panic. Oftentimes our thinking is catastrophic, meaning we may think the worst, most horrible thing will happen. It is important to realize when your thinking is catastrophic since that will be the first step to changing it. There are many ways in which our thinking can be catastrophic. Ten of these ways include

- a thought that something is all good or all bad or that something always or never happens;

- a thought that increases the importance of negative things or decreases the importance of positive things;

- a thought that because we feel something is true, that means it is true;

- a thought that one negative event means all similar events are negative;

- a thought that we or someone else is a bad person, instead of one that just describes a particular behavior that happens;

- a thought that the good parts of something are not important, everyone could do them, or they don't count;

- a thought about the negative thoughts or intentions of others, when there is no evidence to support them;

- a thought that something negative will happen in the future when there is no evidence to support it;

- a thought that you are the reason something went wrong even though it was not actually under your control;

- a thought on how you or others "should" or "ought to" behave or perform. This type of thought is rigid and often unrealistic.

for you to do

Come up with an example of each of the ten types of catastrophic thinking. If the example is a thought you've actually had before, even better.

Catastrophic Thinking	Example
• a thought that something is all good or all bad or that something always or never happens;	
• a thought that increases the importance of negative things or decreases the importance of positive things;	
• a thought that because we feel something is true, that means it is true;	

• a thought that one negative event means all similar events are negative;	
• a thought that we or someone else is a bad person, instead of one that just describes a particular behavior that happens;	
• a thought that the good parts of something are not important, everyone could do them, or they don't count;	
• a thought about the negative thoughts or intentions of others, when there is no evidence to support them;	
• a thought that something negative will happen in the future when there is no evidence to support it;	
• a thought that you are the reason something went wrong even though it was not actually under your control;	
• a thought on how you or others "should" or "ought to" behave or perform. This type of thought is rigid and often unrealistic.	

more to do

For a week, whenever you realize that you have a negative feeling (sad, mad, bad, and so forth), answer this question: What thought(s) came just before that feeling?

As you're doing this throughout the week, try to notice any patterns. People tend to have particular thoughts and types of thoughts that happen often and regularly. Are there any specific thoughts you notice creeping up more frequently than others? If so, write them down, and be on the lookout for them in the future.

_____

_____

_____

_____

_____

_____

from catastrophic to realistic thinking 20

We are only human and cannot change that our brain sometimes offers up catastrophic thoughts. But what we can do is follow up on those thoughts with as many helpful and realistic thoughts as we can think of.

for you to know

Here are some tips to aid you in enhancing your realistic and helpful thinking:

- Don't get mad at yourself for having your initial catastrophic thoughts.

- Come up with as many realistic and helpful thoughts as you can; the more the better.

- If you get stuck, think about what you would tell your best friend or a child. Usually we can be extra creative in coming up with something realistic and helpful for someone else.

- Each thought does not need to make you feel better. Just be creative and come up with as many as you can to increase the likelihood that one or a few may help a little.

- Guess on a 1-to-10 scale how bad you are feeling (10 is the worst), and try to keep telling yourself realistic and helpful things until you get that number down as far as possible. Cutting it in half is a good goal. Consider even a one-point reduction a success.

for you to do

Create a cheat sheet of realistic and helpful thoughts that you may be able to use often. The good news is that there are many realistic and helpful thoughts that can make you feel better in a variety of situations.

In creating your cheat sheet, feel free to use any of the following and add to your list whenever you think of new ones.

I'm only human.

Humans make mistakes.

It's not the end of the world.

No one is focusing on me as much as I am; other people are focused on themselves.

I will learn from the situation what I can and then move forward.

I need to accept the things I cannot change.

I am not choosing to have panic; it's not my fault.

My best is good enough.

It's okay to feel nervous; I am capable of doing what I want to do anyway.

Realistic and Helpful Thoughts Cheat Sheet

_____

_____

_____

_____

_____

_____

_____

_____

_____

_____

_____

more to do

Here you will be using the thoughts you wrote down in step 1 of the "more to do" section in activity 19. For each negative thought, write as many realistic and helpful ones as you can that may make you feel a bit better about that initial thought.

From Catastrophic to Realistic Thinking

_____

_____

_____

_____

_____

_____

_____

_____

_____

_____

it is not only what you say but how you say it 21

It is not only what you say to yourself when attempting to move past panic, but also how you say it that matters. If you yell at yourself harshly to "calm down," you will only feel worse. If you gently encourage yourself to "calm down," you will feel better.

ethan's story

Ethan was having a rough tennis practice. He had a hard time sleeping the night before because he was worried about his finals. He arrived at practice and told himself he would just have to do his best and hoped his tennis performance would not be impacted by his less-than-ideal mental state. Ethan's coach, Fernando, immediately laid into him. He asked him what was wrong with him and questioned his commitment to the sport. He told him that he had other kids that he could be coaching who would not be wasting his time. He ended his rant by informing Ethan that with his lackluster attitude, he would not amount to anything.

for you to do

1. How do you think Ethan is feeling as his coach berates him?

2. How motivated do you think Ethan is to do a good job?

3. How confident do you think Ethan is feeling?

4. How strong and capable do you think Ethan is feeling?

5. How likely do you think it is that Ethan will play well the next time he has a training session with Coach Fernando?

Think of a time in your own life when someone coached you in a harsh and aggressive fashion. How did it make you feel? How motivated for success were you after this interaction?

Now, think of a time when someone coached you in an encouraging, supportive manner. How did it make you feel? How motivated for success were you after this interaction?

What are some of the harsh judgments that you have made of yourself because you struggle with panic? Below is a list of the most common judgments that we hear our clients make about themselves. Check off any harsh judgment that you have made of yourself.

☐ You are such a loser.

☐ There is something wrong with you.

☐ Why can't you just be normal?

☐ You are pathetic.

☐ You are broken.

☐ You are a freak.

☐ There's nothing wrong, yet you're falling apart.

☐ You are weak.

☐ You are defective.

☐ You can't handle life.

If you are experiencing an uncomfortable panic symptom and are receiving a strong (yet inaccurate) signal that you are in danger and you begin yelling at yourself, "You are such a loser. What is wrong with you?" will this likely

a. lead to your panicky moment passing more quickly,

b. lead to your panicky moment lasting longer, or

c. have no impact on your panic?

If you answered B, you are correct. Yelling at yourself to be strong will only make you feel more distress, which will prolong your panic. So, it is time to practice being nice to yourself. You are worthy of kindness and compassion even if you experience occasional panic!

more to do

Think of a self-compassion slogan you can say to yourself when in the midst of panic. What is key is that it must be authentic. If you tell yourself, "You are strong and brave" but don't believe it, it won't do any good. Here are a few slogans our clients have used in the past:

- Everybody struggles sometimes, and this is my struggle.

- I may not be perfect, but I am a good person.

- Having panic does not make me broken; it just makes me human.

Now, create a self-compassion slogan that you can offer yourself when in the midst of panic.

_____

_____

For the next week, anytime you experience a panicky moment, complete the chart below. If you need more room, you can download additional copies of this chart at http://www.newharbinger.com/32219.

Date and Time	Description of Panicky Moment	Self-Compassion Slogan Used	Level of Self-Compassion (0–10)

22 growing bored of panic

The human brain can grow bored with anything, even the sensations and thoughts associated with panic. The key ingredient in growing bored of something is repetition. When we reexperience something enough times, eventually our brain loses interest and seeks out new stimuli to explore.

carly's story

Carly was thrilled to finally be taking drivers education, as she was now one step closer to being a driver. She was confident that driving would come easily to her, given how desperately she wanted the ability to go where she wants to go, when she wants to go. Drivers education was a piece of cake for the first few weeks, and Carly felt she could practically taste the freedom of the open road. All was well until her driving instructor introduced parallel parking. As soon as Carly would attempt to parallel park, she would freeze up, have a hard time thinking clearly, and feel defeated, all at once. She was beginning to think she would have to depend on the mercy of others for rides for the rest of her life until she finally had a breakthrough moment. Her driving instructor shared with her a technique that assisted her in parallel parking with ease. Weeks later, she felt not only confident in her parallel parking abilities but also bored with the prospect of any additional parallel parking practice.

for you to do

Think of something that has been hard or scary for you to do in the past that you now see as easy (for example riding a bike or jumping off a diving board). How strong was your feeling of fear when you first had to tackle it? How strong is your feeling of fear now that you have accomplished the task? Keep in mind how you initially believed that it was too hard and would never get easier, but now you can barely remember why it was scary in the beginning. Now think about the scary things that you face in the present.

more to do

Now think of something that you have had a strong positive feeling toward that has grown boring over time. For example, a video game that seemed so exciting at first, but after you played it everyday for months, it became boring. The purpose of this activity is to recognize that strong feelings, whether positive or negative, change over time with repeated exposure.

Look through a newspaper or news site and find an article or an image that creates a strong emotional response in you. Note the level of your initial emotional reaction (on a scale of 0 to 10, 10 being the strongest). Find an article or image that creates an emotional reaction of at least a 5. Next, reread the article or continue to look at the image enough times that your emotional reaction goes down to near 1. How long did it take for your mind to shift from reacting strongly to barely reacting at all?

23 discomfort vs. anxiety

It is important to tease apart how uncomfortable you find a sensation from how much anxiety a sensation creates. You may stub your toe and feel extreme discomfort but experience no anxiety. We can develop the same relationship with panic sensations.

for you to know

There is a difference between how uncomfortable a sensation is and how anxiety-provoking it is. For example, a migraine is really painful and unpleasant, but you don't necessarily fear it. Jumping into a freezing cold pool creates an unpleasant sensation, but the cold water isn't scary. Therefore, it is important for you to tease out what things just feel uncomfortable or unpleasant and what is actually scary. This will help you manage your reactions to panic sensations so you break the cycle of fearing the feelings of panic, which only brings on more panic. Remember, you can expect to feel discomfort in many situations, but this discomfort need not elicit anxiety.

for you to do

Think of five situations where you may experience discomfort, but the discomfort would not be associated with anxiety.

1. _____

_____

2. _____

_____

3. _____

_____

4. _____

_____

5. _____

_____

more to do

Over the next week, using the chart below—which you can download more copies of at http://www.newharbinger.com/32219—keep track of any situations that are uncomfortable but *not* panic-related situations (for example, stubbed toe, paper cut, mosquito bite). On a scale of 1 to 10, write down how uncomfortable the sensations you feel are and how much anxiety they evoke.

Date and Time	Description of Sensation	Discomfort Level (1–10)	Anxiety Level (1–10)

In addition, over the next week, using the chart below, track all panic sensations you experience. (Download more copies of the chart, if you need them, at http://www .newharbinger.com/32219.) Note the level of discomfort you feel as well as the level of anxiety you feel.

Date and Time	Description of Panic Sensation	Discomfort Level (1–10)	Anxiety Level (1–10)

Do you notice a difference in the association between discomfort and anxiety ratings in the first chart versus the second? Do you see a pattern where there is a big difference between your discomfort ratings and your panic ratings for non-panic-related sensations? In contrast, are your discomfort ratings similar to your anxiety ratings for the panic-sensation chart? The more we can get your brain to separate how uncomfortable a panic sensation is from how anxiety-provoking a panic sensation is, the greater the freedom from panic that you will achieve.

24 help from the sidelines: calling all panic coaches

If you have yet to call upon a panic coach for assistance, now is as good a time as any to obtain some help from the sidelines as you face panic head on.

for you to know

In the next few exercises, we will begin the practice of *interoceptive exposure*. This simply means intentionally bringing on the sensations of panic in order to teach your brain that panic is uncomfortable but not dangerous. The challenge with interoceptive exposure is that it sounds a lot scarier than it actually is. We don't want to lose you at this critical point in your journey past panic.

The practice of intentionally bringing on panic sensations is as counterintuitive as sticking your hand in a hot stove. In both cases, every cell in your body wants to pull away and avoid the threat. But a hot stove is truly dangerous while a panic attack is simply a pesky false alarm. Although you now may intellectually understand that panic sensations are uncomfortable but not dangerous, you may still need an external source of support to help you complete the interoceptive exposure exercises described in the next few exercises. (You made a list of these people in activity 17.) A good panic coach can be anyone in your life whom you trust and can rely upon to assist you in pushing forward.

for you to do

Can you think of something in your life you have accomplished that you would not have been able to do if you had not had someone on the sidelines cheering you on?

How did this coach help you?

_____

_____

In what form did he or she support you?

_____

_____

What did you value most about this relationship?

_____

_____

more to do

Have you reached out to your panic coach yet?

Yes   No

If you have not reached out to your panic coach, what has gotten in the way of your doing it?

- Have you been able to identify a panic coach? If you have not been able to identify a panic coach, is there someone in your life that you trust enough to have him or her help you brainstorm to identify someone who could serve as your panic coach? We are never nearly alone as we feel. We can guarantee that there is someone in your life who can be a helpful panic coach for you.

- Have you decided what you can say to the panic coach to explain to him or her what you are experiencing and what you need from him or her? (Hint: You can always provide your coach with this workbook and highlight sections that speak to your experience and needs.)

- Do you feel as if you should be strong enough to get through this on your own? The very act of asking for help is the first step in moving past panic. By doing this, you are saying that you can handle being vulnerable and imperfect, which moving through panic entails.

- Is there anything else that is getting in the way of your reaching out to your panic coach? Whatever it is, we suggest you address it. You deserve support and encouragement, and you shouldn't have to take this journey alone.

Once you have a panic coach in place, we suggest you do the following:

- Talk to your coach about your panic-fighting plan.

- Review with him or her all of your homework assignments.

- Brainstorm a list of ways he or she can hold you accountable for the tasks you set for yourself.

- Ask whether he or she could send text reminders to you.

- Ask whether he or she could join you as you practice.

- Ask whether you could send an e-mail with a daily update of what you have worked on.

- Ask whether you could schedule a weekly check-in time.

- Ask whether he or she would be willing to remind you of your panic-fighting mantra when you need to hear it.

25 what is your panic recipe?

The key to moving past panic is to learn to no longer fear the sensations of panic. The way we teach our brain that it need not fear panic and that panic is uncomfortable but not dangerous is through the practice of interoceptive exposure.

for you to know

Interoceptive exposure is a fancy name for a simple concept and involves practicing feeling the sensations of panic over and over again until your brain grows bored of these feelings. The first step in conducting interoceptive exposure is to figure out which sensations of panic you fear. If you remember in activity 3, we reviewed the sensations of panic and you filled out a chart similar to the one you'll find in this section. Take a few moments and fill out this chart again. Have there been any shifts? Are there any new sensations causing you discomfort or any old sensations that are no longer bugging you?

Sensations of Panic	Yes or No	Level of Anxiety Associated with the Feeling (0–10)
Foggy head, difficulty concentrating, or light-headedness		
Feeling weird and out of it		
Distorted vision		
Difficulty breathing		
Feelings of suffocation		
Increased heart rate or tightness in your chest		
Upset stomach		
Tingly, cold hands or feet		
Feeling shaky		
Feeling hot or increased sweating		
Other:		

What we are now going to do is attempt to recreate these sensations, in order to practice having them. Yes, you read that correctly. We are going to assist you in experiencing the sensations of panic enough times that before you know it, your brain will grow bored of them.

Listed in the table that follows are different exercises that others have found helpful in conjuring up paniclike feelings.

Panic Sensations	Exercises to Bring on Feeling (Choose one per row.)	Anticipated Anxiety Rating (0–10)	Discomfort Rating (0–10)	Actual Anxiety Rating (0–10)	Similarity to Panic Rating (0–10)
Foggy head, difficulty concentrating, or light-headedness	Hyperventilate for one minute (breathe loudly and rapidly, similar to a panting dog), at a rate of approximately forty-five breaths per minute.				
	Place your head between your legs for one minute, then quickly sit up.				
Feeling weird and out of it	Stare up at the sky and think about the solar system and how teeny-tiny you truly are.				
	Stare up at the sky and picture yourself standing on the Earth as it rotates around the Sun.				
	Stand still, in a dark room, blindfolded, with noise-cancellation headphones on for five minutes.				
	Think to yourself, "Who am I? Who am I?" over and over again for five minutes.				
Distorted vision	Stare intensely at your eyes in a mirror for one minute.				
	Stare at a dot on the wall for one minute.				
	Spin rapidly in a circle, with your eyes open wearing dark sunglasses indoors, for one minute.				
	Stare at a lightbulb for one minute and then attempt to read.				

Panic Sensations	Exercises to Bring on Feeling (Choose one per row.)	Anticipated Anxiety Rating (0–10)	Discomfort Rating (0–10)	Actual Anxiety Rating (0–10)	Similarity to Panic Rating (0–10)
Difficulty breathing	Hold your nose and breathe through a thin straw for one minute.				
Feelings of suffocation	Wear a tight turtleneck. Spend one minute in a small space, such as a closet.				
Increased heart rate or tightness in your chest	Drink a coffee or espresso or other caffeine-based drink. Run up and down stairs for five minutes. Do five minutes of moderately intensive cardiovascular exercise.				
Upset stomach	Think about something upsetting or write down upsetting thoughts for five minutes. Do twenty jumping jacks after a meal.				
Tingly, cold hands or feet	Hyperventilate for one minute (breathe loudly and rapidly, similar to a panting dog) at a rate of approximately forty-five breaths per minute.				
Feeling shaky	Tense all of your muscles and hold the tension for one minute.				

99

Panic Sensations	Exercises to Bring on Feeling (Choose one per row.)	Anticipated Anxiety Rating (0–10)	Discomfort Rating (0–10)	Actual Anxiety Rating (0–10)	Similarity to Panic Rating (0–10)
Feeling hot, or increased sweating	Wear a jacket or wrap yourself in a blanket in a hot room. Run up and down stairs for five minutes. Do five minutes of moderately intensive cardiovascular exercise.				
Feeling dizzy	Spin around really fast for one minute. Spin around in a chair for one minute.				
Other sensation not listed:	How can you creatively conjure up this feeling? (Hint: What activities have you avoided for fear it will bring on these feelings?)				

for you to do

1. Don't panic (although it's fine if you do panic, because you are stronger than panic and can handle whatever panic throws your way)! You do not have to do all of the interoceptive exercises at one time. This activity is meant to be completed over a few days. We recommend spending thirty minutes a day working through this exercise. Also, you should now be in contact with your coach, and this would be a fantastic time to ask for some assistance from the sidelines.

2. Assess your anticipated anxiety for each sensation. How much anxiety does the thought of engaging in the exercise and intentionally trying to bring up the specified feeling cause?

3. Follow the exercise description and intentionally try to bring on the panic feeling. The goal is to do all exercises, even if you assigned an anticipated anxiety level of 0. Sometimes we think something won't make us anxious, but it completely shoots up our anxiety. And other times we think something is going to freak us out, but it is actually a piece of cake. Start with the sensations that you rated the lowest, and each day move on to more anxiety-provoking exposures.

4. After you follow the instructions to bring on the panic feeling, fill out how uncomfortable you found the feeling as well as how anxious the exercise made you feel. Finally, fill out how similar to the experience of panic the feeling was.

5. Remember, it is normal to feel anxious about the thought of intentionally bringing on the sensations of panic. Keep in mind the reason you are completing this exercise: you are teaching your brain that panic is nothing more than a nuisance. It is not dangerous, and it can't hurt you. Once your brain learns this, it will no longer panic about panic and the panic cycle will be broken once and for all. Which means less panic in your life!

more to do

1. Circle the activities in the chart that caused you an anxiety rating of above 0.

2. Now that you have seen the standard list, let's get creative. What sensations does this list not mention that you fear? What other situations have you avoided recently for fear they would trigger panic sensations? Figuring out the situations that you have avoided will help you figure out what other sensations scare you and the kind of circumstances that may bring them on. Add those situations to the list. While panic is common and a lot of people fear similar sensations and situations, panic also likes to show its uniqueness. It is important to tap into all parts of your panic, even if a feeling was not listed.

3. Create your own panic hierarchy. Make a new list of panic sensations, starting with the least anxiety-provoking one and building up to the most anxiety-provoking one.

My Panic Hierarchy

Exercise	Associated Panic Sensation	Rating
		1
		2
		3
		4
		5
		6
		7
		8
		9
		10

26 reward check-in

Not only is now the perfect time to get some TLC from a panic coach, it is also a fabulous time to reward yourself for your panic-extinguishing hard work.

for you to know

You now understand that you must bring on panic sensations in the short term to experience less panic in the long term. Knowing that you will benefit in the long term for short-term discomfort is motivating. But what is also motivating are *rewards*—desired stuff. Short-term rewards sweeten the deal a bit and make the spoonful of "panic medicine" go down a bit more easily.

for you to do

When you are paid for a job, there is a clear reward structure. You may get paid by the hour or by the day or by the project. Whatever the salary structure, you know before you begin the gig how you will get paid. So how are you going to pay yourself for your panic work? We recommend paying yourself for each panic-fighting task you complete. Every time you engage in a panic treatment exercise, you should give yourself a point.

Go back through each activity of this workbook and give yourself a point for each one you have completed. How many points do you have so far?

more to do

Brainstorm a list of dream rewards. Don't let practical realities get in the way of your list. Do you fantasize about seeing your favorite band perform but don't have the funds for a ticket? Put it on the list. Would you love to take a cross-country road trip with your best friend but feel like your panic would never let you accomplish it? Put that down as well. Dream big!

Now for each item, decide how many panic-fighting points it will take to earn it.

Reward	Number of Points

Next, talk to trusted family members or friends and see if they can sponsor you in this mission. Perhaps they would be eager to put money into a pot to assist you in getting paid for your panic-extinguishing hard work.

Now, decide how you will track the points you earn. For example, some of our clients keep track of their points on a chart that they post on their family refrigerator to remind their family of the progress they are making. Others track their points in a notebook or create a note for point tracking in their phone. It does not matter how you track your points. What is more important is that you do it. Don't just think about rewarding yourself for your hard work; truly reward yourself!

27 time to head to the panic gym

The practice of interoceptive exposure is similar to lifting weights at the gym. Every time you do an exposure exercise, you get stronger and less afraid of panicky sensations.

for you to know

In activity 25, you determined which sensations of panic bug you the most and played around with different exercises to recreate these sensations. Now, your goal is to expose yourself to these sensations over and over again until your brain grows bored of them. The level of anxiety each sensation elicited will impact how long it takes for your brain to grow bored of it.

For those sensations that you rated at a 1 or 2, your brain is already quite used to them and does not find them particularly attention grabbing. In contrast, for the sensations you rated as a 5 or above, your brain is still quite reactive to these sensations and interprets them as dangerous. The way to get your brain to not freak out about these sensations is to practice experiencing them several times a day, over the course of a week, until your anxiety rating for each sensation is near 0.

As discussed earlier, it is important to differentiate discomfort from anxiety. When we practice interoceptive exposure exercises with our clients, we too find many of the sensations uncomfortable. We may rate the discomfort associated with hyperventilating as an 8 but the anxiety associated with hyperventilating as a 0.

You don't need to keep practicing until your discomfort rating goes down to 0 because that will never happen for many of these sensations, and it's not the goal of this practice. You just need to practice experiencing these sensations until your anxiety rating goes down to 0.

for you to do

Pop Quiz

Question: Why are you torturing yourself and intentionally practicing experiencing the sensations of panic?

Answer Choices:

a. You are a masochist, and you enjoy making yourself miserable.

b. You're not—you give up and might as well accept that the rest of your life will be filled with anxiety and suffering.

c. You are training your brain to get bored of the sensations associated with panic so that it stops panicking about panic.

If you answered c, give yourself a gold star. If you answered a or b, go back and read this section over again!

more to do

In the chart below, rank the exercises that caused you anxiety, from lowest anxiety to highest anxiety. Your job is to continue to practice each exercise until it no longer elicits anxiety. We recommend you practice these exercises for fifteen minutes in the morning and fifteen minutes in the evening and continue to work on each exercise until all anxiety ratings get down to 0. Additional copies of this chart, if you need them, are available at http://www.newharbinger.com/32219; see the very back of this book for details.

Note that on average, this process takes our clients less than one week.

Interoceptive Exposure Practice Log

Date and Time	Interoceptive Exercise	Discomfort Rating (0–10)	Anxiety Rating (0–10)

leaning in to the panic 28

Panic will pass more quickly if you open yourself up fully and without defense to the sensations that surface. Similar to only sticking your toes into a cold pool, you will get used to the cold pool much more quickly if you jump in, dunk your head, and fully submerge yourself into the water.

evan and zoe

Dr. K's two young children were complaining that their throats hurt. Dr. K took them to their pediatrician to get strep tests. As the nurse approached her son, Evan, he calmly opened his mouth, and seconds later the strep test was over. When it came time for Dr. K's daughter, Zoe, to have her strep test, she ran out of the exam room and attempted to leave the office building. She needed to be carried back into the exam room and held down for the nurse to give the strep test. As the nurse approached Zoe, she attempted to wiggle her way loose, and she kicked and screamed. Finally, fifteen minutes later, the strep test was complete. So, Evan and Zoe both experienced the same procedure. But Evan experienced a good deal less suffering than Zoe because he calmly moved through the discomfort instead of fighting it.

for you to do

- Can you think of a time you fought against doing something that you dreaded, even though you knew it was inevitable you would have to eventually do it?

- Can you think of a time you accepted and flowed with doing something that you dreaded because you knew it was inevitable that you would have to do it?

- Which situation caused you more suffering?

- Which situation used up more of your energy?

more to do

Imagine yourself feeling flooded with panic sensations. Your job is to position your body to fight as hard as you can to *not* have these sensations. What does your body feel like? Where do you feel tension? Where are your shoulders? Draw a picture of yourself fighting the sensations of panic.

When you are practicing interoceptive exposure exercises—or if you are just experiencing out-of-the-blue panic sensations—your job is to try to open yourself up as fully as you can to the sensations instead of fighting them.

29 are you starting to feel anxious? good!

When you can get yourself to experience panic or when panic shows up by itself, it is actually a *good* thing. The more intensely you allow yourself to experience panic, the quicker you will move through and soon past panic disorder.

for you to know

When we are in session with clients and they say, "I am beginning to feel panicky," we reply, "Great! Now we can get to work." We, as anxiety specialists, are panic detectives, and our job is to figure out where panic and anxiety live, and then to do everything in our power to help bring up the feelings and thoughts associated with anxiety so our clients can practice moving through them instead of avoiding them.

Given that you are your own anxiety coach (plus we hope you have followed our advice and found a trusted loved one to assist you from the sidelines), it is your job to develop a fascination with the experience of panic. We want you to get curious and approach anxiety as a specimen you are passionate about examining. By doing so, you are actively rewiring your brain to no longer fear the sensations of panic and anxiety.

for you to do

How can you remind yourself that the more panic you can bring on, the better? One of our clients, Daniel, would tell himself, "short-term pain, long-term gain" and remind himself that the more anxiety he could generate and practice moving through, the quicker he could free himself from panic.

Write down a reminder that resonates with you and put it in the notes section of your phone, keep it on an index card, or write it on your shoe. It does not matter where you keep it, as long as you keep it handy. There is nothing intuitive about the concept of experiencing panic sensations as a good thing, so you are going to need an external reminder of it.

The next time panic surfaces unexpectedly, use your reminder to tell yourself that even when panic arises out of the blue, it is still a good practice opportunity. Daniel used this reminder when he started feeling anxious: "This panicky moment is one more teaching opportunity for my brain. If I can show my brain that it can handle feeling weird and funky when I am out in public, it will learn to no longer freak out about these sensations."

more to do

- Think of an event where you felt very anxious. What do you remember about that day? How vividly can you recall the little details of the day?

- Now think of an event where you did not feel much of an emotional reaction. Perhaps it was driving to work or eating breakfast or brushing your teeth before bed. How much can you remember about this moment of your life? How vividly can you recall the details of this event?

If you want to teach your brain something new (in this case that panic is uncomfortable but not dangerous), is it better to feel a stronger emotional reaction or a neutral emotional reaction?

To teach your brain to respond differently to panicky sensations, we must first get things cooking! If you can get yourself to feel panicky through engaging in interoceptive exposure or if panic decides to show up unannounced, the stage is now set for your brain to learn something new. This is the perfect opportunity to teach your brain that it need not fear panic, and that panic is uncomfortable but not dangerous.

adjust your breathing, adjust your panic 30

You are finally ready to be granted a secret weapon to decrease your panic symptoms: slow breathing. Slow breathing is a tool we only provide to those ready to use it wisely, so congratulations on making it this far in your journey!

for you to know

In the first few sessions of panic treatment, we always ask our clients what they have tried so far to manage their panic symptoms. One of the most common responses we hear is, "I have tried relaxation exercises and focusing on my breath, but they didn't work." In fact, many of our clients tell us that trying to relax only made them feel more anxious. We call this phenomena "relaxation-induced anxiety." If an armed gunman were standing beside you, shouting that you must calm down or else he will shoot, how would you feel? How likely would it be that you would be able to get your body to relax? When we feel desperate to relax or calm down, as though our life depends on it, of course we only end up feeling more anxious. But if we can adopt an open and flexible attitude and tell ourselves, "I would like to calm down, but I don't *need* to calm down," then we increase the likelihood that we will be able to relax.

The most powerful technique to calm down your body is slow breathing. Slow breathing is as simple as it sounds. All you need to do, to take the wind out of the sails of a brewing panic attack, is to engage in five minutes of slow breathing. By engaging in slow, deep breathing, you will send the signal to your brain "the coast is clear; we are not in danger." When you calm down your body, you will also calm down your brain. Just as it defies the laws of gravity for a car to be standing still and driving 100 miles an hour, it is also physically impossible to have a panic attack and simultaneously engage in slow breathing.

To engage in slow breathing, just follow these five simple steps:

1. Breathe in through your nose for three seconds.

2. Hold your breath for three seconds.

3. Breathe out though your mouth for three seconds.

4. Hold your breath for three seconds.

5. Repeat (ideally twenty-five times or for five minutes).

for you to do

In order for slow breathing to be a tool, readily available for your use when you are experiencing panic symptoms, it is best to first practice slow breathing in nonpanicky situations. For the next week, practice slow breathing twice a day, once in the morning and once in the evening, for five minutes, and complete the log below.

What you will need:

- A quiet place. The good news about slow breathing is that you can use this tool anywhere at any time; but for practice purposes, it is best to find a quiet environment where you can focus your attention on your breath.

- A timer. Set the timer on your phone (or any other timer) for five minutes. What is most important is that your mind is not focusing on when this exercise will be over. That is what we have timers for.

Day and Time	Before Slow Breathing Anxiety Rating (1–10)	After Slow Breathing Anxiety Rating (1–10)	Notes
Day 1 Morning			
Day 1 Evening			
Day 2 Morning			
Day 2 Evening			
Day 3 Morning			
Day 3 Evening			
Day 4 Morning			
Day 4 Evening			

Day and Time	Before Slow Breathing Anxiety Rating (1–10)	After Slow Breathing Anxiety Rating (1–10)	Notes
Day 5 Morning			
Day 5 Evening			
Day 6 Morning			
Day 6 Evening			
Day 7 Morning			
Day 7 Evening			

more to do

Some people find it challenging to practice slow breathing because their brain quickly wanders off to different topics, or because the very act of focusing on the breath makes them so hyperaware of this basic body function that their breathing becomes forced and tight. If you notice you are struggling with either of these problems, it may be helpful to use a visual cue, such as the one below, to keep you grounded on the slow breathing exercise.

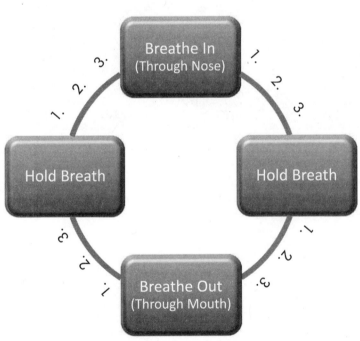

1. Set a timer for five minutes.

2. As you are breathing in for three seconds, rest your finger on the "breathe in" square on the diagram.

3. As you are holding your breath for three seconds, rest your finger on the "hold breath" square.

4. As you are breathing out for three seconds, rest your finger on the "breathe out" square.

5. As you are holding your breath for three seconds, rest your finger on the "hold breath" square.

6. Repeat until the timer goes off.

Now, it is time to take this slow breathing tool on the road and use it when you notice panic symptoms bubbling up. The sooner you take the wind out of the sails of a panic attack, the better. So, the next time you feel a panicky sensation or think a panicky thought, practice five minutes of slow breathing. You will find that your body and mind settle down after this time-out.

In order to know what is and what is not working for you, we recommend that for the next week you fill out the log below every time you have a panicky moment and then engage in five minutes of slow breathing. If you need more space, you can download a copy of this chart at http://www.newharbinger.com/32219.

Day and Time	Situation (Where am I and what am I doing?)	Before Slow Breathing Anxiety Level (1–10)	After Slow Breathing Anxiety Level (1–10)

distress-busting exercises 31

for you to know

Sometimes things just feel too hard, and the most immediate goal is just to get through the moment. In those instances, the most effective way to turn down the volume on your emotional discomfort is to focus outward. There is a time for contemplation and reflection, and there is a time for distraction. When you are in extreme emotional distress, it is most likely not the best time to sit around thinking about yourself. The trick is to learn how to *force* yourself to focus *outward* in moments of unbearable emotional distress. You can focus on the sky, you can focus on a chair, you can focus on your dog, or you can focus on a speck of lint. It does not matter what you focus on as long as it is not on your own thoughts or feelings.

for you to do

After you review the many different options below, select a few you think will work best for you, and memorize those choices. This way, if you are in a situation where you are experiencing severe emotional distress, you will already have decided on a few go-to distress management solutions. Remember that these are only some ideas, and you are welcome to think of your own. The possibilities are endless.

- Count every object you see or every little part of an object.

- Label the different colors you see around you.

- Label object names (chair, window, and so on).

- Identify different shapes you see around you.

- Rip up a piece of paper into small pieces.

- Play with an object that can move (such as a squishy ball, piece of paper, or paperclip).

- If you enjoy something (watching TV, reading, playing videogames) and you have access to it, go ahead.

- Doodle.

- Use your five senses to describe what is going on around you. Use as much detail as you can in your descriptions to really get into the surroundings and out of your head. For example, you could say in your head, "I see a blue couch with white squares on it. I hear a fan. I smell strong honey-scented perfume."

- For each object you see, think of all the ways that object could be used.

These distress-busting ideas focus on what's happening *now*, right this moment. If your mind wanders to the past (triggering feelings of guilt, shame, regret, or anger) or if your mind wanders to the future (triggering worry), try to bring your mind back by refocusing on the present. The trick with these ideas is to get as lost in the current moment as possible. Try not to judge whether you are doing something right. The only goal is to get so involved in the here and now that you are able to handle your distress and give your brain a break from feeling intense anxiety. When you use a strategy during times of distress, feel free to continue using the strategy for as long or short a period of time as you would like. There is no right length of time to use it. Most people like to use one of them until they feel a bit calmer and better able to handle their next move.

more to do

Practice all of the above ideas. You might actually like some ideas that you thought you wouldn't, and you might not like some that you thought you would. It is fine to practice these either at a time when you are feeling distress or at a time when you are not.

32 what do you want your life to be about?

When panic first surfaces, it is easy for life to become about striving to not have panic. Now that you are investing less energy in fighting with panic, it's time to explore what else you want your life to be about.

for you to know

One of the key ways to move past panic is to engage in meaningful living. It is difficult but important work to pull your mind away from reviewing prior panic moments and assessing for the potential of future panic moments, and instead to live fully in the moment. In order to do this, you must first determine what you value and what you would like your life to be about. Unlike goals, values cannot be achieved. They are there simply to guide your behaviors in the right direction.

for you to do

Below are different aspects of life that people value. If one of these is not important to you, you are welcome to skip it. Also, if we have left out a category that is important to you, please feel free to add it.

Circle any of the values that are important to you personally. You are also welcome to edit any of the prewritten ones.

- Friendships

    * Being a good friend

    * Being there for others when they need me

    * Putting effort toward my friendships

    * Allowing friends to help me when I need them

    * Other: _____

- Family relationships

    * Being a nice person toward my family

    * Helping my family

    * Being a good listener

    * Developing strong bonds with them

    * Other: _____

- Significant other relationship

    * Being selfless

    * Being a good significant other

    * Being there for him or her whenever possible

    * Increasing his or her happiness

    * Other: _____

- School

  - *   Being a good student
  - *   Doing my best
  - *   Being willing to try things that are hard
  - *   Being social with others (in class, during free periods)
  - *   Other: _____

- Hobbies

  - *   Trying to do my best
  - *   Taking on challenges
  - *   Being willing to make mistakes or look silly
  - *   Sticking with things even when they're hard
  - *   Other: _____

- Leisure

  - *   Valuing leisure activities as important
  - *   Having the ability to relax fully without electronics
  - *   Being willing to do what's necessary to allow my mind to clear (such as writing down thoughts to deal with later)
  - *   Other: _____

- Work

  - *   Being a hard worker
  - *   Being a punctual person
  - *   Having a can-do attitude
  - *   Other: _____

- Health and fitness

    * Being someone who works out often

    * Being someone who eats healthy

    * Being someone who eats in moderation

    * Other: _____

- Community and volunteer service

    * Helping others when I see them in need

    * Donating when I can

    * Considering how my actions affect others

    * Other:_____

- Relationship with myself, self-esteem, and self-worth

    * Being kind to myself

    * Being patient with myself

    * Believing in myself

    * Other: _____

- Character, integrity, and ethics

    * Doing the right thing

    * Standing up for what I believe in

    * Sacrificing myself for someone else

    * Other: _____

- Self-improvement, growth, and new experiences

  * Continuously trying to learn something new

  * Constantly seeking new experiences

  * Taking on challenges

  * Other: _____

- Spirituality

  * Feeling connected to organized ideology

  * Feeling connected to my own ideology

  * Continually nurturing ideology

  * Other: _____

more to do

Ask yourself whether a particular behavior moves you toward or away from your values and then act accordingly without letting panic stop you. For the following behaviors, write "yes" if you believe that behavior falls in line with the values you circled above, and write "no" if you believe it does not fall in line with the values circled above.

- Staying at home instead of going to my friend's birthday party: _____.

- Stopping myself from yelling at my brother because I'm in a bad mood: _____

- Going to a concert with my boyfriend even though I feel afraid: _____

- Rushing through my test so I can avoid the crowded hallways after the bell rings: _____

- Skipping tennis tryouts because I'm self-conscious about my serve: _____

- Deciding to work through the weekend because I feel uncomfortable wasting time: _____

- Deciding to keep my opinions to myself at work because I sweat when I speak: _____

- Leaving the gym when I see someone whom I feel awkward around: _____

- Taking the time to separate my recycling even though I feel so busy: _____

- Deciding to focus on what I got right instead of wrong on my math test: _____

- Ignoring a girl bullying another girl because I get nervous speaking up: _____

- Going indoor skydiving for the first time with my friend even though it's scary: _____

- Skipping religious holiday services because the crowds make me uncomfortable: _____

33 exposing yourself to valued living

To fully reclaim your life, you must try to do things that you value despite panic sensations occasionally surfacing. When you live fully, you experience life as meaningful despite moments of discomfort.

for you to know

Now that you are clear about the life you would like to live, how are you going to follow through with this vision? Panic may come and go, but your values are consistent over time. Living a satisfying life requires staying on track and continuing to move in the direction of your values, even if panic occasionally comes along for the ride. The key to moving from vision to fruition is to develop a solid plan of attack.

for you to do

- What does valued living mean to you?

_____

_____

_____

_____

- What do you want your life to be about?

  _____

  _____

  _____

  _____

- What activities provide you with a sense of vitality and purpose?

  _____

  _____

  _____

  _____

- What activities do you engage in that leave you feeling empty and restless?

  _____

  _____

  _____

  _____

- If you had a magic wand and could make all panic and anxiety disappear, what activites would you engage in? How would you fill your time?

_____

_____

_____

_____

- If you could create the life of your dreams, what would you be doing in ten years? How old would you be? Where would you be living? What would you be doing? Whom would you be spending your time with? What do you look like in this image?

_____

_____

_____

_____

- What are some ways you can reward yourself for continuing to move forward in the direction of your values, even when panic shows up and attempts to take you off course?

_____

_____

_____

_____

more to do

Using the chart below, fill in all the tasks and activities, no matter how small, that you would like to engage in this week that move you in the direction of your values. Only include items that you may have difficulty engaging in due to panic.

Throughout the week, if you are able to do the tasks and activities you have written, then congratulate yourself and circle them. If you can't do something, just try to focus on the ones that you did.

Unlike values, which are never "achieved," these goals should be concrete and achievable.

Here are just a few examples of what you can include. Looking back at your values from the previous activity should help give you more ideas.

Self-care: Showering; eating healthy, nutritious meals

Health and fitness: Going to my doctor's appointment, going to the gym

School: Getting there on time in the morning, going to each class, participating in class, talking to someone in class, getting help from the teacher for the upcoming exam

Activities: Attending the activity, participating in the activity the entire time

Family: Talking to my family member, speaking nicely to my brother

Friends: Calling a friend I haven't seen in awhile, going with a friend to a party

Life Sphere	Behavioral Goals	Predicted Anxiety	Date Accomplished	Actual Anxiety
Self-Care				
Health and Fitness				
School				
Career Readiness				
Family				
Friendships				
Dating				
Spiritual Life				
Community Service and Activism				
Other				

track your progress 34

When panic symptoms momentarily resurface, it is easy to feel disheartened, as though no progress has been made and that you are exactly back to where you started. In reality, the panic dance is two steps forward, one step back.

for you to know

As you can tell, managing your panic is a process. Thanks to the work you have done so far, you are now more engaged in your life, and the panic is losing increasing amounts of control over your behavior. You are learning to be the boss of your panic. However, it may still creep back in on occasion and attempt to reclaim important terrain in your life. This is a normal part of the process. It is important to remember that your success is not defined by the presence of panicky thoughts or feelings, but rather by the way that you choose to respond to panicky thoughts and feelings. It is also possible that as some situations are becoming easier to face, others are becoming more difficult. This happens for various reasons. First of all, as you move up your panic hierarchy, you are facing the situations that have caused more intense feelings or avoidance. Additionally, your panic is starting to panic that it is losing its prioritized place in your life! The less that you respond to it, the less important it becomes. This phenomenon is great for you but bad for your panic. It is feeling lost and confused and will do anything to try to weasel its way back into your brain and your life! The good thing is that now you are armed with knowledge and evidence that you can face tough situations without their resulting in danger. You now know that even if you feel anxious, the discomfort will soon pass if you don't run away. Pat yourself on the back for all of the progress that you have made. And remember, progress does not mean being panic-free; it means experiencing freedom to live your life despite panic's occasionally rearing its annoying head.

for you to do

This is a great point in your panic-management program to assess your gains as well as the situations and feelings that still cause you distress.

Remember when you first opened this book? You were probably scared, skeptical, and filled with dread. Well, here you are, thirty-four exercises later. You made it! Let's revisit the assessment that you took when you started using this workbook. Answer the following questions based on how you feel today.

For the following questions, provide a rating of 0 to 10 (0 being not at all, 10 being extreme).

_____ In the past week, how uncomfortable did panic sensations make you?

_____ How much distress do you feel about having panic symptoms?

_____ How much do you avoid activities and other aspects of life not to experience panic?

_____ How would you rate your overall life satisfaction?

Now that you have assessed how panic is impacting your current functioning, go back and compare your answers to the answers you gave in activity 1. Are they different? How different are they? How have things changed? Do you have a different perspective on panic now?

Graph It Out

On the blank line graph below, plot your ratings for discomfort, distress, avoidance, and life satisfaction to compare your activity 1 answers with your activity 34 answers.

10	———————————————————————————
9	———————————————————————————
8	———————————————————————————
7	———————————————————————————
6	———————————————————————————
5	———————————————————————————
4	———————————————————————————
3	———————————————————————————
2	———————————————————————————
1	———————————————————————————
0	———————————————————————————

Activity 1 Discomfort   Activity 34 Discomfort   Activity 1 Distress   Activity 34 Distress   Activity 1 Avoidance   Activity 34 Avoidance   Activity 1 Life Satisfaction   Activity 34 Life Satisfaction

more to do

Now that you have assessed your overall changes in panic symptoms and panic management since day one, complete this quick assessment in various situations. Rate your discomfort, distress, avoidance, and life satisfaction when you are the middle of having a panic attack, using the chart below as a guide. Are your ratings of your panic feelings any less than they would have been initially? Additionally, complete the questions when you are feeling really good.

	Rating When Having a Panic Attack (0–10)	Rating When Feeling Good (0–10)
Discomfort		
Distress		
Avoidance		
Life Satisfaction		

Notice how the way that you feel in the moment isn't an accurate representation of your whole life. It just represents one moment in time.

You are constantly evolving as an individual, which means that your panic may still be changing as well. However, with continued perseverance and exposure, you will get better and better at catching panic early, and extinguishing it before it wreaks havoc in your life.

for you to know

In the last exercise you tracked your progress from day one until now. You recognized your strengths and your capabilities. You are also aware that panic likes to play games and will constantly be vying for a place in your life. As you have learned throughout this book, your best defense against panic is exposure and facing your fear head on. In this activity, your job is to determine where panic is still hiding in your mind and in your life. It is important to evaluate how much more work you still need to do in order to reclaim what is rightfully yours! Remember, even though you may still have work to do, you have made so much progress. The existence of panic in different aspects of your life isn't a sign of failure. It is simply a sign of being human.

for you to do

Have you ever played Where's Waldo? Well, we are going to play a game of Where's Panic? The chart below shows different spheres of life. For each section, we want you to take a moment to think about and then jot down how panic is showing up and impacting that area of functioning.

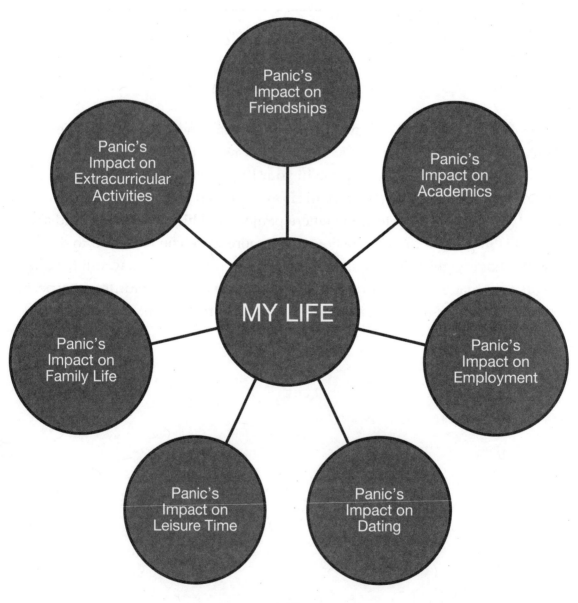

Over the next few days, write down any panic symptoms that still occur as well as any situations that you find yourself avoiding. Assign each feeling or situation a rating that defines how intense the feeling of panic or avoidance seems. Again, this activity is not meant to be discouraging. It is okay for you to still be experiencing discomfort. Take note of how many fewer sensations you are feeling and how many more situations you are conquering. Also evaluate whether the ratings that you assign are less than they would have been in the past.

Day and Time	Situation	Panic Sensations	Anxiety Rating (0–10)

more to do

Now that you have a list of sensations and situations that are still causing discomfort, draw a pie chart. Assign a percentage rating to how much you are in control of your life and what percentage panic is still calling the shots. Here's an example:

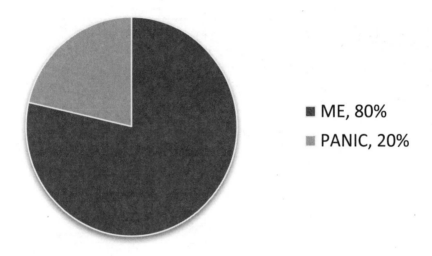

■ ME, 80%
■ PANIC, 20%

Once you assess how much panic is impacting the different areas of your life, it will be easier to see how far you have come and that you can push past the remaining panic that is stubbornly striving to hold its ground.

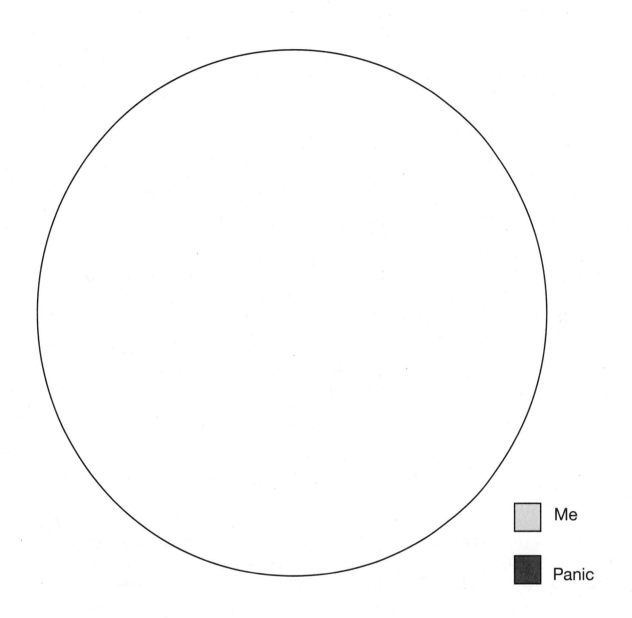

36 define your remaining steps past panic

Now that you know how much panic is left and where it is hiding, let's make a plan to tackle it! You are so close to taking full control back from panic.

for you to know

Remember how far you have come and how daunting any progress initially seemed. You are over the hump, and moving past the final remnants of panic can feel exhilarating. In order to do this, it is important to be just as systematic and consistent as you have been in the past. You may feel like slacking off at times now that you are feeling better. While you do deserve a break, taking one now will just give the panic a chance to slowly try to invade your space again.

for you to do

Take a look at your list from the last exercise. Document your interpretation of your panic sensations (as you did in activity 3). Use the evidence that you have accumulated over the course of completing the activities in this book to challenge the beliefs that you have about the danger or meaning of these symptoms. Looking back at the activities that you avoided, what could you have done differently or what could you have said to yourself to push yourself to participate in the activities despite feeling uncomfortable? The point of this exercise is not to make you feel bad about not perfectly managing your panic. Panic has a habit of increasing its intensity right as you are about to walk out the door, and it is okay if you aren't always able to push through it. However, now that the situation has passed, you can use all of your newfound knowledge and tools to figure out how you can respond differently the next time.

Situation	Panic Sensations	Anxiety Rating (0–10)	Catastrophic Interpretations of Sensations	More Realistic Interpretation of Sensations	How else could I have managed my panic?

more to do

Now it is time to put all of these ideas into action! For each sensation and situation that you wrote down, think of a way to challenge it in the next few days. For the sensations, make an interoceptive exposure schedule. Perform the exposures repeatedly at home until you become bored of the way you feel! Depending on the number of exposures left, you can break them down over a few days in order to make the process less daunting.

With respect to the situations, look at your schedule for the week. Figure out how you can try to put yourself in the same or similar situations. Plan each exposure exercise in advance. You might even put them in your phone or computer calendars and set alerts to make sure that you follow through.

when all else fails, 37
do the opposite

Sometimes even the best-laid plans can backfire. We can make list after list and set multiple reminders to follow through and still not do the things we know are good for us. But have no fear! There is always a way to get back on track and spontaneously kick panic to the curb. A no-fail way to put panic in its place and show it that you are the boss of your own life is to always *do the opposite* of what panic asks of you! Remember opposite day as a kid? If someone says it's wrong, it's really right. Someone tells you yes, he or she means no. Fun, right? Well, now you get to play that game with your panic! Whatever it tells you to do, automatically do the opposite. If it tells you to avoid something, you should go, go, go! If it tells you not to do something because it may bring on scary sensations, purposely do it!

for you to know

I know you may be about ready to do the opposite of what this book is telling you, and you may be about ready to shut it. Please don't! It is hard to do the opposite especially when the consequences seem so risky. However, remember, you have learned that just because panic tells you something, doesn't mean it is true. You have done interoceptive exposures, and you are still here to tell about it. You have participated in situations that seemed impossible, and you came out on the other side! You have been doing the opposite the whole time without even realizing it. Now you just want to make a conscious effort to do the opposite of what panic asks of you every day instead of just in planned situations. Make it a habit!

for you to do

Imagine what it would be like to do the opposite of what your parents, siblings, teachers, and coaches tell you to do. Imagine how it would feel to follow your own convictions even when others try to shut you down. How would you feel if you asked a sibling to borrow a shirt and he or she said no and then you went and wore it anyway? What if you asked your parents if you could go out tonight, they say no, and you go anyway? How would you feel? Just a little caveat: you can't do these things to your parents, sibling, teachers, and coaches. The authors of this book are not promoting disobedience. Rather, it's that we are human, and we know how it feels to be told no and how righteous it would feel to do what we want anyway. The good part is that when it comes to your panic, you can be disrespectful. This is one of the few situations in life where it is not only okay, but it is actually fantastic to not do what you are told. Whenever your panic tells you to do or not to do something, remember how good it feels to be able to do what *you* want when *you* want!

more to do

Pull out the competition chart from activity 13, of you versus your panic. Remember how you earned points every time you didn't listen to your panic. Now you are going to continue to earn points for spontaneously rebelling against it. Set up your competition and keep track of the points you earn for doing the opposite of what panic demands of you. See who wins!

Panic loves it when you let your guard down and forget about it. Panic is like a sneaky burglar who watches the neighborhood to see who is away on vacation so it can climb through an unlocked window and forage for jewelry and electronics.

ethan's story, continued

Ethan was so proud of himself. He made it through ten weeks of therapy for panic disorder, and he finally felt like his old self. He could barely remember the guy who was avoiding parties and requesting rides from his parents to school because he felt too shaky to drive. He had kicked panic's butt through hard work and commitment to get his life back.

When he first started therapy, he was dreading attending sessions because at his appointments he would have to talk about his panicky thoughts and feelings. Now, he was starting to dread therapy because all this panic talk had grown boring. There were so many other things Ethan would rather do than work on his panic. His therapist had suggested they check in once a month to stay on top of panic. But Ethan was determined to move on from this emotionally exhausting chapter in his life. For Ethan, this meant no more working on panic.

Weeks and then months went by, and Ethan was fully back in his life. One day, while studying for the ACTs, Ethan's vision felt a bit off. He had never worn glasses but thought perhaps all the studying was impacting his vision. He went for an eye exam, and his vision was still 20/20. He felt relieved for a short while but couldn't seem to shake the thought that his vision was off and something felt not quite right. He began skipping certain assignments that entailed a lot of reading for fear it would bring up the strange feeling. He next began putting his head down whenever he had "the feeling." Soon, "the feeling" seemed to be showing up more and more. After several doctors ruled out any medical causes for the uncomfortable, strange feeling, Ethan had an aha moment. It was panic showing up in a new form. His first round of panic had involved tightness in his chest and his heart beating rapidly. And now he was bothered by strange sensations in his head. So the feelings were different, but his reactions to the feelings (his fear, his avoidance, and the deep sense of dread) were the same. He may have forgotten about panic, but panic did not return the favor and forget about him.

for you to do

It is quite understandable that you no longer want to work on panic once you are feeling better. The list below highlights comments our clients have made regarding continuing to work on panic once they feel practically back to "their old selves."

Check off all the sentiments that you relate to.

☐ I have wasted too much time with panic and don't want to give it any more of my energy.

☐ I am so sick of thinking about panic.

☐ I want to be like everyone else and not have to work on myself.

☐ I am better now and want to focus on my life, not panic.

☐ I have no energy left to fight panic.

How would you put into words how you feel about continuing to "work on panic" now that you are feeling better?

_____

Why would we recommend you continue to work on panic (in teeny, tiny ways), even though you are starting to feel better?

a. Because we are mean.

b. Because we are trying to torture you.

c. Because you can prevent panic from growing big and taking over your life again if you actively take yourself a bit out of your comfort zone, every day, in some small way.

more to do

Because it is all too easy to forget about working on panic when life gets better, it is helpful to write a note to yourself to remind yourself why it is important to move through versus try to avoid feelings of anxiety.

Here is a sample note, which one of our clients wrote to herself:

> When in the grips of panic, all I want to do is run and hide. I would do anything and give up anything to make the discomfort stop. Panic came on slowly and quickly robbed me of the things most important to me—my family, my friends, my career aspirations. I refuse to let it do that again. I will open myself up to the discomfort in order to live life to its fullest.

Now, you give it a try. There are no right words. All that matters is that you craft a note that speaks to you. You can even draw a picture or make a collage or write a poem. Be creative and speak from your heart.

_____

_____

_____

_____

The way to prevent future panic is to inoculate yourself with small daily doses of panicky thoughts and feelings. Similar to taking vitamin C daily to prevent a cold or going to the gym every day to maintain physical fitness, doing tiny, daily panic exposures will keep away the big, messy panic episodes.

hailey's story

Hailey was starting to feel so much better. She could barely remember what life was like when it was dictated by panic's never-ending demands for avoidance and escape. She was tempted to take a break from her panic-fighting work now that she had some hard-earned relief, but then she thought of her recent diet debacle.

Hailey had gained fifteen pounds during her freshman year of college. None of her favorite clothing fit her, and she just was not feeling comfortable in her own skin. She decided to go on a hard-core health kick. She signed up for an intense workout boot camp. She did a juice cleanse. Then she even went gluten-free. Ten weeks later she was thrilled to be at her goal weight. She was exhausted from all of the dieting and exercise and glad for life to return to normal. All was good until she got back on the scale a few months later. She was shocked to see that she had put back on the fifteen pounds that she had worked so hard to take off. She then realized that what she needed was a life-style change, not a one-time health kick. Moving forward she would prioritize healthy eating and exercise over the long haul, not just as a short-term strategy to take off a few pounds.

A small poke at panic a day is enough to show it you are now in charge of your life. If you spend around five minutes a day allowing yourself to experience panicky thoughts and feelings, you should have no problem keeping panic away.

for you to do

What self-care activities do you do on a daily basis, as part of your routine?

- ☐ Take vitamins

- ☐ Brush teeth

- ☐ Wash face

- ☐ Shower

- ☐ Put on deodorant

- ☐ Shave

- ☐ Get dressed

- ☐ Eat

- ☐ Drink water

- ☐ Sleep

- ☐ Exercise

- ☐ Other: _____

Can you make room on your list of daily self-care activities for a small panic-busting exercise?

- ☐ Yes

- ☐ No

Review the list below of small panic exposures that our clients have found helpful in warding of future panic episodes. Check off the ones that may induce small bursts of panicky sensations in you.

- ☐ Anything from the Panic Gym checklist in activity 27

- ☐ Drinking a shot of espresso

- ☐ Giving a speech

- ☐ Saying something awkward

- ☐ Going out with your hair messed up

- ☐ Talking about a topic you know little about

- ☐ Asking for a job application

- ☐ Asking a teacher for assistance

- ☐ Asking a new friend to get together

- ☐ Asking someone on a date

- ☐ Taking a train ride

- ☐ Riding on an airplane

- ☐ Riding a roller coaster

Next, come up with a list of a few mini panic-busting exercises that you can engage in on a daily basis. This list need not be exhaustive. You will change over time, and new issues will emerge that make you feel panicky. Just keep this list handy, and when you stumble upon something new in life that causes you distress and pushes you out of your comfort zone, update it with the new life challenge. Every day is a good day to shrink panic down to a shadow of its former size.

My Panic-Busting Exercise List

1. _____

2. _____

3. _____

4. _____

5. _____

6. _____

7. _____

8. _____

9. _____

10. _____

more to do

Like any form of self-care, such as dieting or exercise, we all know what is good for us, but doing these things can feel like such hard, exhausting work.

1. What will most likely get in the way of your doing a daily panic-busting exercise?

    _____

2. Who can support you with this initiative? Can you discuss this exercise with your coach?

    _____

3. What reminders can you place in your environment to remind yourself to do a small panic-fighting exposure every day?

    _____

4. Can you think of a mantra to remind yourself why it is important to keep engaging in daily panic-busting exposures?

    _____

5. What will be the best time of day for you to engage in a daily panic-busting exposure?

    _____

Remember, the goal is for you to work your panic-fighting muscles a little bit every day.

40 advice to and from fellow travelers

Panic has a way of robbing you of your sense of connection. Panic may tell you that you are the only one who struggles with strange and uncomfortable thoughts and feelings. It may tell you that no one could possibly understand how you feel. Unfortunately, it is this isolation from your life and from your loved ones that allows panic to strengthen its tight hold on you. The truth is you are not alone.

for you to know

We run panic disorder support groups at our anxiety treatment centers. Our clients are often resistant to attending these meetings. They feel ashamed to discuss their panic with others. They fear they will be judged and looked down upon if they open up about their panic. After a decent amount of encouragement (and a dash of tough love), we are often able to get our clients to attend one of our panic-support groups.

Something truly beautiful happens when our clients struggling with panic and anxiety attend a support group. They quickly realize they are not alone. Group participants always have similar reactions. They report back something along the lines of, "I can't believe these fantastic people who seem to have it all and look so normal on the outside actually experience the same challenges that I do."

What participants in panic support groups also realize is they are so much better at giving advice and offering panic-fighting tips to others than they are to themselves. They are able to compassionately remind other group members that there is nothing wrong with them but that they have an overreactive alarm system in their brain. But when it comes to their own symptoms, they quickly revert back to "I should be stronger" or "There must be something wrong with me if I am having these problems." In other words, it is often easier to offer effective support to others than it is to ourselves.

for you to do

We asked some of the participants in our teen panic support group to offer advice to our readers. They exceeded our expectations with their words of wisdom.

Panic sucks, but it does not last forever. Just because you feel awful now does not mean you will always feel awful.

Through fighting panic, I learned just how strong I am. I now have a sense of maturity and purpose at twenty-one that I never would have had if I did not have to work so hard on learning to deal with panic.

When I first started struggling with panic, it felt dangerous to tell anyone how I was feeling. I feared they would think I was crazy and lock me up, or at the very least they would look back at me with a mix of confusion and pity. But now I so glad I found the strength to get help. I deserve to have a fun life versus being stuck in a panic prison.

When my friends get caught up in drama and nonsense, I am able to keep focused on what is most important to me. I have learned that I am not going to let anything get in the way of my living my life...not panic and not high school politics.

You are not a freak just because you struggle with panic.

Panic may come and go, but you can handle whatever it throws your way. You are stronger than you think.

Talk to someone about your panic. You will feel such relief when someone nods their head and tells you that they understand how you feel.

1. What advice would you offer other teens struggling with panic?

_____

_____

_____

_____

2. We want to know! We learn so much from our fabulous clients, and we want to learn from you. Share your panic-fighting tips with us by sending an email to drdebra@lightonanxiety.com.

more to do

Think about your first panic attack. Where were you? What were you doing? Really put yourself there. What were you wearing? Were you sitting or standing? Once you have a solid image in your mind of yourself having your first panic attack, imagine that present-day you enters this scenario, with all of your new panic-management tools.

- What would you tell yourself about what was happening to you?

- What tips would you offer yourself to better manage the moment?

- Can you feel compassion and offer support to this frightened, confused you?

The key to moving past panic is to compassionately coach yourself through a panicky moment. You now have all the tools you need to become your own panic coach. So be kind to yourself. You deserve it!

Debra Kissen, PhD, MHSA, is clinical director of the Light on Anxiety Treatment Center. Kissen specializes in cognitive behavioral therapy (CBT) for anxiety disorders, and also has a special interest in the principles of mindfulness and their application for anxiety disorders.

Bari Goldman Cohen, PhD, is a licensed clinical psychologist who specializes in cognitive behavioral therapy (CBT) and anxiety disorders. She works with individuals of all ages, including children, adolescents, adults, and older adults.

Kathi Fine Abitbol, PhD, is a licensed clinical psychologist and clinical director of the North Shore Anxiety Treatment Center. She specializes in using cognitive behavioral therapy (CBT) to treat anxiety disorders and related concerns. Abitbol works with clients of all ages.

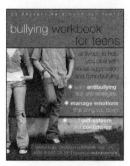

Register your **new harbinger** titles for additional benefits!

When you register your **new harbinger** title—purchased in any format, from any source—you get access to benefits like the following:

- Downloadable accessories like printable worksheets and extra content

- Instructional videos and audio files

- Information about updates, corrections, and new editions

Not every title has accessories, but we're adding new material all the time.

Access free accessories in 3 easy steps:

1. Sign in at NewHarbinger.com (or **register** to create an account).

2. Click on **register a book**. Search for your title and click the **register** button when it appears.

3. Click on the **book cover or title** to go to its details page. Click on **accessories** to view and access files.

That's all there is to it!

If you need help, visit:

NewHarbinger.com/accessories

new harbinger
CELEBRATING
40 YEARS